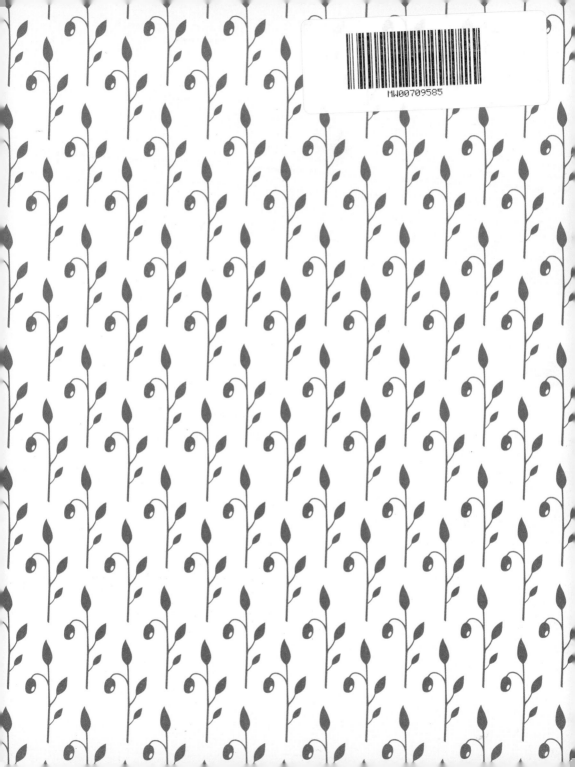

GEORGE CALOMBARIS

George Calombaris was voted one of the 'Top 40 Chefs of Influence in the World' in 2004 by *The Global Food and Wine Magazine*, and he continues to live up to this acclaim. He owns seven restaurants in Melbourne – The Press Club, Hellenic Republic, Maha, P M 24, Little Press & Cellar, St Katherine's and Mama Baba – as well as consulting for The Belvedere Club restaurant in Mykonos, Greece. George is the author of *Georgie Porgie*, *The Press Club: Modern Greek Cookery* and *Greek Cookery from the Hellenic Heart*, and co-author of *Cook With Us* and *Your Place or Mine?*.

GEORGE CALOMBARIS

LANTERN
an imprint of
PENGUIN BOOKS

STARTERS, SIDES AND SMALL BITES

MAINS

SWEETS

BASICS

STARTERS, SIDES AND SMALL BITES

Taramosalata

This is the real stuff – not pink, but white. My brother-in-law Dave recently rang me to tell me my godson, Michael, who means the world to me, was in the garage dipping popcorn into a tub of taramosalata. How cool is that? I am so proud!

4 slices white bread, crusts removed
300 ml water, to cover
½ small onion, roughly chopped
100 g salted white cod roe paste (see page 141)
2 tablespoons lemon juice
550 ml olive oil, plus extra for drizzling
sea salt flakes
sourdough bread, to serve

1 Put the bread into a bowl, then cover with water and soak for 15 minutes. Remove the bread and squeeze out any excess water. Set aside.

2 Blend the onion in a food processor until smooth. Add the squeezed bread and blend until smooth. Add the cod roe paste and lemon juice to the food processor and blend once again until smooth. While the motor is running, slowly drizzle in the olive oil, a little at a time. (The aim is to create an emulsion with the consistency of mayonnaise.) Taste to check the seasoning and add a little salt if necessary.

3 Place in a bowl, drizzle with some more olive oil, then serve with bread for dipping. (Leftover taramosalata will keep in an airtight container in the fridge for up to 1 week.)

Avocado tzatziki

This dip is made by emulsifying flavoured oil with avocado. Make the flavoured oil the day before so it can infuse overnight. The dip is delicious served with tiny crisp fried whitebait, as I've done here, and is also great spooned over barbecued or grilled chicken or fish.

1 teaspoon ground cumin
1 teaspoon ground turmeric
100 ml extra virgin olive oil
3 avocados
juice of ½ lemon
1 clove garlic, crushed
¼ cup (70 g) natural Greek-style yoghurt
sea salt flakes

FRIED WHITEBAIT (OPTIONAL)
vegetable oil, for deep-frying
500 g whitebait
plain flour, for dusting

1 Heat the ground cumin and turmeric in a small dry frying pan over low heat for 30 seconds or until fragrant. Remove the pan from the heat, then add the olive oil and set aside to infuse for 30 minutes. Strain the oil through coffee filter paper (or strong paper towel) placed over a bowl. Set aside.

2 Halve the avocados, and remove the seeds. Remove the flesh and put it into a food processor. Add the lemon juice and garlic and blend until smooth. While the motor is running, slowly add the flavoured oil and blend to a puree.

3 Transfer the avocado puree to a bowl and fold in the yoghurt. Season to taste with salt and set aside.

4 If making the fried whitebait, preheat oil for deep-frying in a deep-fryer or heavy-based saucepan to 180°C (or until a cube of bread browns in 15 seconds).

5 Toss the whitebait in flour to coat, then carefully fry in batches for 2 minutes or until crisp. Remove the whitebait from the deep-fryer and drain on paper towel.

6 Serve the avocado tzatziki – with the fried whitebait, if desired.

Skordalia

When I was growing up, this was the sort of food that made regular appearances on our dining table. Making it always brings back memories of Dad sitting down at the table to a big bowl of skordalia, homemade baked beans, crusty bread and a glass of white wine; that was often his lunch. Such memories are the essence of what good food is all about.

3 large sebago potatoes (about 750 g)
400 g rock salt
1 head garlic, cloves separated, peeled
1 cup (250 ml) milk
sea salt flakes
200 ml extra virgin olive oil, plus extra
    for drizzling
1 tablespoon lemon juice, to taste
crusty bread, to serve

1 Preheat the oven to 180°C fan-forced (200°C conventional).

2 Bake the potatoes in a roasting pan on a bed of rock salt for 50 minutes or until tender when pierced with a skewer. When cool enough to handle, peel the potatoes and set aside.

3 Meanwhile, place the garlic and milk in a small saucepan. Bring just to the boil over medium–high heat, then reduce the heat to low and simmer until the garlic is tender, 12–15 minutes. Set aside.

4 Pound the garlic and 1 teaspoon salt with a large mortar and pestle to form a paste. Push the potatoes through a potato ricer or sieve into the mortar. Add ¼ cup (60 ml) of the garlic-infused milk. Using the pestle, mash the potatoes until smooth, adding extra milk as needed.

5 Gradually pour in the olive oil in a slow, steady stream, stirring constantly with the pestle until the mixture has the consistency of thick mayonnaise. Stir in lemon juice to taste.

6 Transfer the skordalia to a shallow bowl and drizzle with extra olive oil. Serve immediately with crusty bread. (Skordalia will keep in an airtight container in the fridge for up to 2 days.)

Greek-style scrambled eggs

Hot scrambled eggs with a juicy homemade Greek-style tomato sauce on toast is the type of simple fare I'd come home to after school. Lucky me! The tomato sauce can be stored in an airtight container in the fridge for up to five days, and it is also delicious served alongside grilled meat or fish.

5 roma (plum) tomatoes (or
   1 × 400 g tin crushed tomato)
ice cubes
100 ml extra virgin olive oil
1 onion, thinly sliced
4 cloves garlic, thinly sliced
1 tablespoon tomato paste (puree)
3 stems thyme
sea salt flakes and freshly ground
   black pepper
4 slices sourdough, toasted
8 eggs
⅓ cup (80 ml) pouring cream
20 g unsalted butter
100 g feta, crumbled
roughly chopped flat-leaf parsley,
   to serve

1 Cut a small cross in the base of the tomatoes, then plunge into a pan of boiling water until the skins start to peel at the cross, about 30 seconds. Plunge into iced water, then peel off the skins, cut in half and remove the seeds. Roughly chop and set aside. Heat the olive oil in a saucepan over medium heat. Add the onion and cook until translucent, about 6 minutes. Reduce the heat to low–medium, then add the garlic and cook until the onion is light golden, about 15 minutes. Stir in the tomato, tomato paste and thyme. Reduce the heat to low and cover with a piece of baking paper (cartouche, see page 140). Cook for 35 minutes or until the sauce has a jam-like consistency, stirring occasionally to prevent it from sticking to the base of the pan. Season to taste with salt and pepper and remove the thyme. Set aside.

2 Have the toasted sourdough ready and keep warm. Place a large non-stick frying pan over medium–high heat. Gently whisk the eggs and cream in a bowl until lightly beaten. Melt the butter in the pan. Pour in the egg mixture, then, using a spatula, move the egg mixture around the pan. When it has almost set, gently stir in the tomato sauce to just combine.

3 Spoon the scrambled eggs and tomato sauce over the toast and place on warmed plates. Sprinkle with crumbled feta and parsley. Serve immediately.

Cauliflower-cheese croquettes

Cauliflower and cheese is one of those classic flavour combinations that often reminds people of their childhood. Here I've transformed it in a sophisticated and quirky way, if I say so myself. For a Greek touch, I've used kefalograviera cheese (see page 141), as well as the semi-soft sheep's or goat's milk cheese manouri, both of which can be found in Greek food stores and good delis.

2 cups (500 ml) milk
500 g cauliflower, thinly sliced
sea salt flakes
3 gold-strength gelatine leaves
    (see page 140)
⅔ cup (100 g) plain flour
3 eggs
2 cups (140 g) fresh breadcrumbs
vegetable oil, for deep-frying
lemon cheeks, to serve

BECHAMEL SAUCE
50 g unsalted butter
50 g plain flour
350 ml reserved hot milk (from
    cooking the cauliflower)
50 g grated kefalograviera cheese
    (see page 141) or use parmesan
50 g grated manouri (see above)
30 g grated cheddar

1 Put the milk and cauliflower into a saucepan, then season with salt and quickly bring to a simmer over medium–high heat. Cook the cauliflower for 5 minutes or until just cooked through. Drain well, then set the cauliflower aside and reserve the hot milk for the bechamel sauce (see below).

2 Place the gelatine leaves in a small bowl of cold water and leave for 5 minutes to soften.

3 Meanwhile, for the bechamel sauce, melt the butter in a saucepan over medium heat, then stir in the flour. Cook for 2 minutes, stirring continuously. Reduce the heat to low. Slowly pour in 350 ml of the reserved hot milk, stirring continuously, until the mixture is smooth and lump-free. Remove from the heat and stir in the cheeses until melted.

4 Drain the gelatine leaves and squeeze out excess water. Stir the gelatine into the hot bechamel sauce until completely dissolved. Gently fold in the cauliflower. Spread the mixture in a baking dish to form a 2 cm-deep layer. Cover with plastic film and refrigerate for 4 hours or until set.

5 Preheat the oven to 100°C fan-forced (120°C conventional).

6 Place the flour in a shallow bowl. Beat the eggs in a second bowl, then put the breadcrumbs into a third bowl. Heat enough oil for deep-frying in a deep-fryer or heavy-based saucepan to 180°C (or until a cube of bread browns in 15 seconds).

7 Roll heaped teaspoonfuls of the cauliflower mixture into balls. Roll each ball first in flour, shaking off excess, then dip into the egg to coat all over and roll evenly in breadcrumbs. Deep-fry the croquettes in batches until golden brown and crisp. Remove with a wire basket or slotted spoon and drain on paper towel. Transfer to a baking tray and keep warm in the oven while you cook the remaining croquettes. Serve immediately with lemon cheeks to the side.

Chilli-salted beans

Eat these instead of salted nuts with an aperitif and really get your tastebuds ready for a big dinner. Just remember to soak the beans the day before. Don't salt the water when cooking them as it toughens the skins so they take longer to cook.

50 g dried butter or borlotti beans
50 g dried black-eyed beans
50 g dried cannellini beans
50 g dried chick peas
sea salt flakes
vegetable oil, for deep-frying

SPICY SALT
⅔ cup (100 g) plain flour
1 teaspoon ground cinnamon
2 teaspoons cayenne pepper
2 teaspoons table salt

1 Soak the dried beans together in a bowl of cold water overnight.

2 Drain the beans and put into a large saucepan, then cover with cold water. Bring to the boil, then reduce the heat to low and cook for 45 minutes or until tender. Season with salt, then cook for another minute. Drain the beans, then transfer to a baking tray lined with paper towel and put into the fridge to dry for at least 2 hours.

3 Meanwhile, for the spicy salt, mix together the flour, cinnamon, cayenne pepper and salt.

4 Heat oil for deep-frying in a deep-fryer or heavy-based saucepan to 190°C (or until a cube of bread browns in 12 seconds). Working in small batches, dust the dried beans with the spicy salt and deep-fry for 2–3 minutes or until golden and crisp. Drain on paper towel. Sprinkle with a little salt and serve immediately.

Golden thread prawns with cocktail sauce

This party snack is a real crowd-pleaser. In my early days as a chef I would make a thousand of these a week – but that's my job and I love it! Use an Asian spiral vegetable cutter (see page 140) to make the potato strips.

1 large coliban potato
½ cup (60 g) custard powder
12 large raw prawns, peeled, cleaned,
    with tails intact
vegetable oil, for deep-frying
lime wedges (optional), to serve

COCKTAIL SAUCE
1 cup (250 ml) Mayonnaise (see page 134)
½ cup (125 ml) tomato sauce (ketchup)
1 tablespoon worcestershire sauce
a few drops of tabasco sauce (optional)
juice of 1 lemon

1 Peel the potato and put it into a bowl of water to prevent it from browning. Use an Asian spiral vegetable cutter to make spiral strips of potato.

2 Mix the custard powder with a little water to make a thin paste. Dip the potato strips in the custard mixture and roll the potato around the prawns. Set aside.

3 Meanwhile, for the cocktail sauce, mix the mayonnaise, tomato sauce, Worcestershire sauce, Tabasco (if using) and lemon juice in a small bowl. Adjust the flavours to taste by adding more tomato sauce, Worcestershire sauce, Tabasco and lemon juice, if necessary. Set aside.

4 Preheat oil for deep-frying in a deep-fryer or heavy-based saucepan to 180°C (or until a cube of bread browns in 15 seconds). Deep-fry the potato-wrapped prawns for 4 minutes or until golden brown and crisp. Drain on paper towel, then serve with cocktail sauce for dipping, with lime wedges to the side, if you like.

Salmon and dill gravlax

I think we should all try this classic method for making gravlax, even though it's easy enough to go out and buy it from the supermarket. It is lovely to be able to cure a piece of salmon yourself and show your friends you can do it, and it's just not that hard. You will need to start this the day before you wish to serve it. Gravlax is beautiful served with a little dollop of creme fraiche and a scattering of capers.

1 x 1 kg salmon fillet (1 side)
2 tablespoons cumin seeds
2 tablespoons coriander seeds
1 tablespoon dill seeds
1 tablespoon black peppercorns
3 large handfuls of roughly chopped dill
200 g caster sugar
200 g sea salt flakes

1 Using fish tweezers (see page 140), remove the small pin bones along the centre of the salmon fillet. Wipe the salmon dry with paper towel.

2 Heat the cumin seeds, coriander seeds and dill seeds in a small, dry non-stick frying pan over low–medium heat, tossing the pan occasionally, for 1–2 minutes or until fragrant and lightly toasted. Crush the toasted spices and peppercorns with a mortar and pestle until coarsely ground. Combine the spices with the chopped dill.

3 Lay a large sheet of plastic film on a clean work surface. Combine the salt and sugar and spread half across the centre of the plastic film. Place the salmon, skin-side down, over the salt-sugar mixture. Evenly spread the spice and dill mixture over the top of the salmon and gently pat down. Spread the remaining salt-sugar mixture over the top. Wrap the salmon tightly in the plastic film and transfer to a plastic tray or glass or ceramic dish. Refrigerate for 6 hours, then turn over and refrigerate for another 6 hours.

4 Remove the plastic film, then brush off the excess salt-sugar mixture and dill mixture, which will have turned into mush. Rinse under cold water to remove any remaining salt and herb mixture. Gently pat dry with paper towel.

5 Using a sharp, flexible, long-bladed knife, and starting at the tail-end and working back towards the head-end, cut the fillet on the diagonal into very thin slices. Serve right away or store, wrapped in plastic film, in an airtight container in the fridge for up to 1 week.

Onion and anchovy filo cigars

When you've gone to the trouble of making your own filo pastry it deserves to be filled with something special. You can make this great little starter dish in advance and keep it in the freezer for up to a month. When you have guests coming over you can just pop the cigars on a baking tray in the oven and bake until golden, then serve. And you could always use purchased filo pastry, if you're short of time.

100 ml extra virgin olive oil
1 kg onions, thinly sliced
1 quantity Filo Pastry (see page 135)
200 g unsalted butter, melted, for brushing
**25 anchovy fillets in oil (I use Ortiz brand), halved
    lengthways, drained on paper towel**
icing sugar (optional), for dusting

1 Heat the oil in a large non-stick frying pan over medium–high heat. Add the onion and stir to coat well, then stir occasionally for 10 minutes or until softened. Reduce the heat to low, cover with a sheet of baking paper (cartouche, see page 140) and press it down on the onion. Cook the onion for 25–30 minutes, stirring occasionally to prevent it from sticking to the base of the pan, until it is dark golden and very soft; it should be jam-like. Set aside to cool. (The onion can be stored in an airtight container in the fridge for up to 1 week.)

2 Preheat the oven to 200°C fan-forced (220°C conventional). Have ready 2 baking trays lined with baking paper.

3 Working quickly, cut the filo pastry strips into 15 cm lengths and place on a floured bench, then brush with melted butter. Working with one strip of pastry at a time, place an anchovy piece across one end, then spread a line of onion mixture over the anchovy. Roll the filo into a cigar shape, tucking in the sides as you roll. Brush the outside of the pastry with butter and place the cigar seam-side-down on a prepared baking tray.

4 Bake the cigars until golden and crisp, about 6–8 minutes. Lightly dust with icing sugar (if using) and serve.

Tuna confit with snowpea salad

I'm usually reluctant to cook tuna because I love eating it raw. However, if you do want to cook it the best way is to confit it gently in olive oil spiked with coriander seeds, as I've done here.

3 tablespoons coriander seeds
1 star anise, broken into pieces
3 cups (750 ml) extra virgin olive oil
zest of ½ lemon, in strips, white pith removed
2 × 160 g sashimi-grade tuna loins, trimmed
    into 9 cm × 5 cm × 3 cm pieces
crushed ice
80 g snow peas (mange-tout)
2 tablespoons lemon juice, plus extra if needed
sea salt flakes and freshly ground white pepper
large handful of snowpea (mange-tout) shoots

1 Heat the coriander seeds and star anise in a small, dry non-stick frying pan over low–medium heat, tossing the pan occasionally, for 1–2 minutes or until they are fragrant and lightly toasted. Lightly crush the coriander seeds and star anise with a mortar and pestle.

2 Put 670 ml of the olive oil, the spices and lemon zest into a deep saute pan or heavy-based saucepan on a simmer mat (see page 141) over low heat. Heat the olive oil until it registers 55°C on a sugar thermometer (see page 141). Add the tuna, then cook for 10 minutes: the fish should be rare and translucent in the centre but cooked around the edges. (The olive oil needs to return to 55°C soon after the tuna is added to ensure it cooks evenly, so adjust the heat if required.) Using a slotted spoon, transfer the tuna to paper towel (or a clean tea towel) to drain and leave to cool to room temperature. Strain the coriander seeds from the olive oil and set aside. Discard the oil.

3 Have a bowl of iced water ready. Cook the snow peas in a saucepan of boiling water for 1 minute. Remove with a slotted spoon and plunge into the iced water to stop the cooking process, then drain well and finely shred. Set aside.

4 Put the lemon juice and the remaining 80 ml olive oil in a small bowl and stir to mix well, adding more lemon juice to taste, if desired. Season to taste with salt and pepper.

5 Cut the tuna into 1 cm-thick slices and divide among plates, then top with a small handful of shredded snowpeas and snowpea shoots. Drizzle with the dressing, then sprinkle with the reserved coriander seeds, if desired. Serve immediately.

Grilled mussels with skordalia crust

SERVES 6

Mussels are such a fantastic ingredient: they are cheap, readily available and grown in Australia – and they taste brilliant topped with this garlic-infused crust. This is a great little meze or tapas dish to get your appetite going.

100 ml dry white wine
2 cloves garlic, thinly sliced
3 stems flat-leaf parsley
36 black mussels, bearded, rinsed

SKORDALIA CRUST
2 cups (140 g) fresh breadcrumbs
¼ cup (60 ml) clarified butter (see
    page 140), melted
1 tablespoon finely chopped chives
3 tablespoons finely chopped flat-leaf parsley
sea salt flakes and freshly ground white pepper
½ quantity Skordalia (see page 12)

1 Put the wine, garlic and parsley into a large saucepan, then top with the mussels and cover with the lid. Cook over medium–high heat for 3–5 minutes or until the mussels open, shaking the pan occasionally. Remove from the heat and leave until cool enough to handle.

2 Gently prise open the mussel shells, breaking off and discarding the top shells. Discard any unopened mussels. Separate the mussels from the shell with a small sharp knife, then replace the mussels in their shells.

3 For the skordalia crust, place the breadcrumbs, butter, chives and parsley in a bowl and mix well to combine. Season to taste with salt and pepper. Top each mussel with a teaspoonful of skordalia. Spoon the breadcrumb mixture over to cover well. Place the prepared mussels in a baking dish.

4 Preheat an overhead griller to medium heat. Place the mussels under the griller for 5 minutes or until the crust is golden. Serve immediately.

Beetroot terrine

My head chef at The Press Club, Joe Grbac, cooks this dish for the restaurant and I love it. Beetroot is cheap, versatile and available year-round. I find large beetroot especially gutsy and flavoursome. The terrine needs to set in the fridge overnight.

6 large beetroot (about 6 cm each)
2 cups (500 ml) port
finely grated zest and juice of 2 lemons
juice of 2 oranges
1 cinnamon stick
1 clove
3 tablespoons redcurrant jelly
pinch of cayenne pepper
6 gold-strength gelatine leaves (see page 140)
edible flowers (optional) and sour cream, to serve

1 Preheat the oven to 180°C fan-forced (200°C conventional). Line a 1 litre-capacity terrine mould with plastic film, leaving some overhanging to help lift out the set terrine.

2 Wrap each beetroot in a piece of foil. Bake for 1 hour or until tender when pierced with a knife. When cool enough to handle, using disposable kitchen gloves, peel off the skin (it will slide off easily) and trim the ends of each beetroot. If necessary, trim the sides of the beetroot to fit the width of the terrine mould. Cut the beetroot into 6 mm-thick slices and set aside. Discard the offcuts.

3 Place the port, lemon juice and zest, orange juice, cinnamon, clove, redcurrant jelly and cayenne in a saucepan and bring to a simmer over medium heat. Simmer for 10 minutes or until the liquid has reduced to 2 cups (500 ml). Set aside to cool to room temperature. Strain the liquid through a fine-mesh sieve lined with muslin into a jug, discarding the solids.

4 Soak the gelatine leaves in a bowl of cold water until softened, about 5 minutes. Bring 1 cup (250 ml) of the port mixture to a simmer in a small saucepan, then remove from the heat. Remove the gelatine from the water and squeeze out any excess water. Stir the gelatine into the hot port mixture in the pan until dissolved, then stir into the rest of the port mixture in the jug to combine. Pour a 6 mm-deep layer of the port mixture into the terrine mould. Refrigerate until just set, about 1 hour.

5 Place a layer of sliced beetroot over the set jelly, cutting the pieces to fit where necessary, then pour in enough port mixture to just cover the beetroot. Refrigerate until the jelly has just set, about 1 hour. Repeat this layering process until the terrine mould is full, using all the beetroot and jelly mixture. Cover with plastic film and refrigerate overnight.

6 Remove the top layer of plastic film. Use the overhanging plastic film to lift out the terrine or invert it onto a platter or chopping board, then remove the plastic film. Cut the terrine into 1.5 cm-thick slices, then scatter with edible flowers (if using) and serve with sour cream.

Chicken wing confit with fennel and walnut salad

I think that chicken wings are the yummiest part of the chicken – I just want to lick the bones and extract the flavour from every bit. Served with this crunchy salad, the wings are absolutely delicious.

4 cloves garlic, peeled
100 g sea salt flakes
handful of thyme stems, chopped
2 kg (about 18) chicken wings, wing tips
    removed and discarded
1 litre extra virgin olive oil, plus extra
    as needed
goat's curd and edible flowers (optional),
    to serve

FENNEL AND WALNUT SALAD
100 g walnuts
juice of 1 lemon
¼ cup (60 ml) extra virgin olive oil
1 bulb baby fennel, base trimmed,
    fronds reserved, bulb thinly sliced
sea salt flakes and freshly ground
    white pepper

1 Crush the garlic with 2 teaspoons of the salt using a mortar and pestle. Combine with the remaining salt and thyme in a bowl and mix well. Rub each chicken wing with the salt mixture and place on a plastic tray or ceramic or glass dish large enough to hold them in a single layer. Scatter over any remaining salt mixture. Cover with plastic film and refrigerate for 1 hour.

2 Preheat the oven to 90°C fan-forced (110°C conventional).

3 Rinse the chicken wings under cold running water to remove the salt mixture. Pat the wings dry with paper towel. Holding each side of a wing, spread it open to break the joint (this makes it easier to remove the bones after cooking), then return the wings to their original shape. Place the chicken wings in a large roasting pan snugly, side by side. Pour in enough olive oil to cover completely, then cover the pan tightly with foil.

4 Cook the chicken wings in the oven for 2½ hours or until the meat is tender and pulls away from the bones. Remove from the oven and leave to cool to room temperature.

5 For the fennel and walnut salad, increase the oven temperature to 180°C fan-forced (200°C conventional). Put the walnuts onto a baking tray and toast for 6 minutes or until golden. Set aside. Combine the lemon juice and olive oil in a small bowl, add the fennel and season with salt and pepper.

6 Reduce the oven temperature to 80°C fan-forced (100°C conventional). Drain the chicken wings on paper towel. If desired, carefully push out and discard the large bones from each wing keeping the shape intact. Heat a thin film of olive oil in a large non-stick frying pan over medium–high heat and fry the wings for 2–3 minutes on each side or until golden. Drain on paper towel and keep warm in the oven.

7 Cut each wing in half at the joint. Spread a little goat's curd on each plate, then divide the wings among the plates. Top with the drained fennel and scatter with the walnuts, fennel fronds and edible flowers (if using). Season with salt, drizzle with olive oil and serve.

Chicken liver parfait with samos vin doux jelly

It's very important that all the ingredients for this parfait are at room temperature so that they incorporate and set properly. The jelly not only adds a sweet flavour but also protects the parfait from spoiling due to exposure to oxygen.

5 golden shallots, thinly sliced
1 clove garlic, thinly sliced
100 ml madeira
100 ml port
3 stems thyme
1 fresh bay leaf
5 white peppercorns
250 g unsalted butter, chopped
250 g chicken livers, cleaned and
    all sinew removed
3 eggs, at room temperature
1½ teaspoons table salt
toasted baguette, to serve

SAMOS VIN DOUX JELLY
100 ml samos vin doux (see page 141)
    or sauternes
50 ml water
1½ gold-strength gelatine leaves
    (see page 140)
ice cubes

1 Place the shallot, garlic, madeira, port, thyme, bay leaf and peppercorns in a small saucepan and simmer over low heat for 6–7 minutes or until reduced to ¼ cup (60 ml). Strain through a fine-mesh sieve over a bowl, pressing down on the solids to extract as much flavour as possible. Discard the solids and leave the reduction to cool.

2 Meanwhile, melt the butter in a small saucepan, then leave to cool to room temperature.

3 Preheat the oven to 120°C fan-forced (140°C conventional).

4 Process the livers in a food processor until smooth. Add the eggs, one at a time, and process until well combined, then add the cooled reduction and salt and combine well. Press the mixture through a fine-mesh sieve over a large bowl. Whisk in the butter until well combined. (If the butter sets or curdles the mixture, warm the bowl very gently over a pan of simmering water, whisking continuously until the mixture becomes smooth again.)

5 Divide the mixture among three 300 ml-capacity ramekins. Line a small roasting pan with a piece of cardboard or a tea towel. Place the filled ramekins on top and fill the pan with enough lukewarm water to come halfway up the sides of the moulds. Bake for 35–40 minutes or until just set. (The internal temperature should reach 62°C on a meat thermometer.) Remove the ramekins from the water bath and leave to stand at room temperature for 30 minutes.

6 Meanwhile, for the jelly, bring the wine and water to just below simmering point in a small saucepan over low heat, then remove from the heat. Place the gelatine in a bowl of iced water and soak for 5 minutes or until soft. Squeeze out any excess water, then add the gelatine to the wine mixture and stir until dissolved. Strain through a fine-mesh sieve over a bowl, then leave to stand until cool but not set. Pour 50 ml jelly mixture over the top of each parfait, then refrigerate for 2 hours or until jelly is firm and set.

7 Serve the parfait with slices of toasted baguette and salt.

Caramelised onion scrolls

MAKES 12

When I worked as a second-year apprentice at Le Restaurant in Melbourne, it was my job to make onion scrolls for dinner service. I was always so hungry that I'd eat one as soon as they came out of the oven. Yum!

10 g active dried yeast (see page 141)
100 ml lukewarm water (32°C)
575 g plain flour
45 g caster sugar
2 teaspoons table salt
175 ml milk
230 g unsalted butter, softened,
    plus extra for greasing
sea salt flakes

CARAMELISED ONION
150 ml extra virgin olive oil
1.5 kg onions (about 10), thinly sliced

1 For the onion, heat the olive oil in a large non-stick frying pan over medium–high heat. Add the onion and stir to coat well. Cook for 10 minutes, stirring occasionally until softened. Reduce the heat to low, cover with a sheet of baking paper (cartouche, see page 140) and press it down on the onion. Cook the onion for 25–30 minutes, stirring occasionally to prevent it from sticking to the base of the pan, until it is dark golden and very soft; it should be jam-like. Set aside to cool.

2 Place the yeast, water and 75 g of the flour in the bowl an electric mixer, then stir with a wooden spoon to combine. Cover with plastic film and set aside in a warm spot until the mixture becomes frothy and almost doubles in volume, about 30 minutes. Meanwhile, place the sugar, salt and milk in a small saucepan over low heat until just lukewarm, stirring to dissolve the sugar. Melt 50 g of the butter, then stir into the milk mixture.

3 Add the remaining flour to the yeast mixture, then beat with the dough hook on low speed, slowly adding the milk mixture until incorporated.

Continue mixing just until the dough comes together in one piece; it should feel firm. Transfer the dough to a lightly floured work surface and knead to form a ball. Shape into a 3 cm-thick rectangle. Transfer to a baking tray, cover with plastic film and refrigerate for 2 hours.

4 Roll the dough on a lightly floured bench into a 50 cm × 20 cm rectangle. Evenly spread one-quarter of the softened butter over two-thirds of the dough. Fold the unbuttered third over the middle third, then fold the other side back over on top; like folding a letter into thirds (this is one 'turn' of the dough). Roll to form a 50 cm × 20 cm rectangle. Spread the dough with another quarter of the butter, then fold into thirds and turn it so that the open fold seam is to your left (this is two turns). Transfer the dough to the baking tray, cover with plastic film and refrigerate for 2 hours.

5 Roll the dough out again and repeat the folding and turning process with half of the remaining butter, then refrigerate for 2 hours. Repeat this process a final time, using the remaining butter. (The dough has now been turned 4 times.) Transfer the dough to the baking tray, cover with plastic film and refrigerate for 2 hours.

6 Lightly brush a 12-mould-capacity muffin pan with butter. Roll the dough out on a lightly floured work surface to a 50 cm square. Trim the sides to neaten, then cut into twelve 4 cm-wide strips. Spread one-twelfth of the onion mixture along the length of each strip, then roll into a spiral, swiss-roll style, and transfer to the muffin pan. Cover with plastic film and set aside in a warm place until the dough has nearly doubled, 1½–2 hours.

7 Preheat the oven to 200°C fan-forced (220°C conventional). Put the muffin pan into the oven and immediately reduce the temperature to 180°C fan-forced (200°C). Bake for 15 minutes or until light golden. Cool on a wire rack. Serve warm or at room temperature, sprinkled with salt.

Baked feta souffles with smoked almond and grape vinaigrette

Here I've taken a classic cheese souffle and added a Greek touch with salty feta and a smoky almond and fruity grape vinaigrette, which you can spoon over the top or serve as a small side salad.

olive oil, for cooking
1 small onion, finely chopped
1 teaspoon thyme, chopped
50 g unsalted butter, plus extra soft
   butter for greasing
300 ml milk
60 g plain flour
90 g feta, crumbled
3 egg yolks
4 egg whites
baby mache (lamb's lettuce), to serve

SMOKED ALMOND AND GRAPE VINAIGRETTE
100 g red grapes, washed, halved lengthways
3 small golden shallots, finely chopped
1 tablespoon tomato sauce (ketchup)
1 tablespoon sherry vinegar
⅓ cup (80 ml) extra virgin olive oil
30 g sultanas
30 g smoked almonds, quartered
sea salt flakes

1 Heat a splash of olive oil in a small frying pan, then saute the onion and thyme over medium heat for 5 minutes or until soft. Blend in a small blender.

2 Lightly grease six 250 ml-capacity souffle moulds with butter.

3 Heat the milk in a saucepan over low heat; do not allow it to boil. Melt the butter in another saucepan over medium heat, then add the flour and cook, stirring, for 3 minutes. Gradually add the hot milk, stirring well. Bring to the boil, then simmer for 2 minutes. Add the feta and onion mixture and combine well. Leave to cool slightly, then add the egg yolks and mix thoroughly.

4 Preheat the oven to 150°C fan-forced (170°C conventional).

5 Whisk the egg whites to soft peaks. Fold through the cheese mixture. Fill each mould three-quarters full with the souffle mixture. Place the souffle moulds in a roasting pan, then add enough boiling water to come three-quarters of the way up the sides of the dishes. Carefully transfer the pan to the oven. Bake for 25–30 minutes or until risen and lightly golden.

6 Meanwhile, for the vinaigrette, place the grapes and shallot in a mixing bowl, then add the tomato sauce, sherry vinegar, olive oil, sultanas and almonds and mix together well. Season with salt and set aside.

7 Serve the souffles with the vinaigrette and baby mache.

Tabbouleh with preserved lemon

This is not your traditional tabbouleh, as I use freekeh instead of burghul. The freekeh gives the dish a wonderful chewy texture. Eat it as a meal in itself with a dollop of yoghurt on top or serve it as a side dish for fish or pork.

250 g whole freekeh (see page 140)
1.3 litres water
large handful flat-leaf parsley, finely chopped,
    plus extra sprigs to serve
3 tablespoons finely chopped coriander
40 g raisins
1 preserved lemon quarter (see page 140),
    pulp removed, rind finely chopped
juice of ½ lemon
⅓ cup (80 ml) extra virgin olive oil
sea salt flakes

1 Put the freekeh and water into a saucepan and bring to a simmer over high heat. Reduce the heat to low and cook for 45 minutes or until tender. Spread the freekeh over a baking tray and set aside to cool.

2 Add the parsley, coriander, raisins and preserved lemon to the freekeh. Add the lemon juice and olive oil, then season with salt. Stir to mix. Scatter with extra parsley sprigs. Serve.

Warm salad of squid with chick peas and wild greens

During Lent in Greece it's traditional not to eat seafood containing any blood, so squid is very popular at that time of year. Flash-fried like I've done here, the squid goes really well with lentils, chick peas, vinegar and olive oil to make a really healthy, tasty dish. I like to include amaranth, a leafy vegetable, popular in Greek, Chinese, Central American and Indian cuisines, in this salad.

2 small squid (about 200 g each)
1 carrot, cut into 4 pieces
1 onion, cut into 4 pieces
1 stick celery, cut into 4 pieces
80 g dried puy-style green lentils
1 fresh bay leaf
1 litre cold water
50 ml extra virgin olive oil, plus extra for drizzling
6 leaves Tuscan black cabbage (cavolo nero), washed, trimmed, cut into 4 cm lengths
375 g endive, washed, trimmed, cut into 4 cm lengths
110 g amaranth, washed, trimmed, cut into 4 cm lengths
2 tomatoes, cut into 5 mm dice
90 g tinned chick peas, drained and rinsed
1 tablespoon sherry vinegar
sea salt flakes
baby mache (lamb's lettuce), to serve (optional)

1 To clean the squid, remove tentacles and all parts inside the tubes, including the head, beak and quill, then rinse well. Reserve the tentacles for another use. Cut the tubes into 2 cm pieces. Set aside.

2 Put the carrot, onion, celery, lentils and bay leaf into a saucepan. Cover with the cold water, then simmer over low heat for 40 minutes or until the lentils are tender. Drain the lentils, discarding the vegetables and bay leaf.

3 Heat the olive oil in a large frying pan over high heat. Add the squid and fry for 3 minutes or until golden brown, then add all the greens and cook for 1 minute or until wilted. Add the lentils, tomato and chick peas and fry for another 1 minute. Add the sherry vinegar and drizzle with a little more olive oil.

4 Season to taste with salt, then scatter with mache, if desired. Transfer to plates or shallow bowls and serve.

Mum's rice pilaf

The cheapest and simplest ingredients can create the best dishes. Take this rice pilaf, for example: it is just delicious. Eat any leftovers cold the next day, with some natural yoghurt mixed through.

½ cup (125 ml) olive oil
50 g unsalted butter
1 cup (about 55 g) crushed egg
    vermicelli noodles
1 onion, finely chopped
1 clove garlic, thinly sliced
1 cup (200 g) long-grain rice
2 cups (500 ml) water
sea salt flakes
1 cup (80 g) flaked almonds
freshly ground black pepper
1 cup (150 g) currants
thinly sliced coriander, to serve

1 Heat the olive oil and butter in a large saucepan over medium heat. Fry the crushed noodles for 2–3 minutes or until crisp and browned. Add the onion and garlic and continue to cook for 2–3 minutes or until softened. Add the rice and cook for a further 2 minutes. Pour in the water and season with a pinch of salt. Bring to the boil, then cover with a tight-fitting lid, reduce the heat to the lowest setting and cook for 10 minutes. Remove the pan from the heat and leave to sit with the lid on for another 10 minutes.

2 Meanwhile, preheat the oven to 160°C fan-forced (180°C conventional).

3 Toast the almonds on a baking tray for 5 minutes or until light golden. Set aside.

4 Remove the lid and fluff up the rice with a fork. Season with salt and pepper to taste. Stir through the currants, almonds and coriander. Serve.

Spiced eggplant and tomato with saffron yoghurt

Store this in a jar in the fridge for up to three days, so you can help yourself to a spoonful whenever you like. It's fabulous with barbecued chicken or steak.

2 teaspoons coriander seeds
2 teaspoons cumin seeds
140 ml extra virgin olive oil
2 red onions, thinly sliced
1 clove garlic, thinly sliced
1 × 400 g tin crushed tomato
1 tablespoon sherry vinegar
1 tablespoon tomato paste (puree)
olive oil, for deep-frying
2 eggplants (aubergines), cut into
     2 cm cubes
2 teaspoons sea salt flakes
10 coriander leaves
10 mint leaves

SAFFRON YOGHURT
small pinch of saffron threads
50 ml milk
200 g natural Greek-style yoghurt

1 Preheat the oven to 180°C fan-forced (200°C conventional).

2 Heat the coriander and cumin seeds in a small, dry non-stick frying pan over low–medium heat for 1–2 minutes or until fragrant and lightly toasted. Crush with a mortar and pestle until finely ground.

3 Heat 1 tablespoon of the olive oil in a saucepan over high heat, then add the onion, garlic, coriander seeds and cumin seeds and cook for 4 minutes or until the onion is translucent. Add the tomato, sherry vinegar, tomato paste and remaining olive oil and cook over low heat for 45 minutes.

4 Meanwhile, for the saffron yoghurt, heat the saffron and milk in a small saucepan over low heat for 2 minutes. Set aside for 1 hour to infuse. Add the saffron milk to the yoghurt and mix well. Cover with plastic film and refrigerate.

5 Heat enough olive oil for deep-frying in a large heavy-based saucepan or deep-fryer until it reaches 180°C (or until a cube of bread browns in 15 seconds). Fry the eggplant in batches for 2–3 minutes or until just tender; make sure the oil returns to 180°C before adding the next batch of eggplant. Drain on paper towel.

6 Remove the tomato mixture from the heat and add the eggplant. Season with salt and set aside to cool. Finely shred the coriander and mint, then add to the cooled eggplant mixture. Serve the eggplant with a bowl of saffron yoghurt to the side.

Cypriot grain salad

This recipe comes to you straight from the menu at my restaurant Hellenic Republic. Travis, my head chef, serves up hundreds of portions of this a night. We get inundated with requests for the recipe, so I thought it would be a good opportunity to share it here.

1 cup (165 g) whole freekeh (see
    page 140, or use burghul)
½ cup (100 g) green puy-style lentils
1 teaspoon cumin seeds
1 cup (280 g) natural Greek-style yoghurt
1 tablespoon honey
2 tablespoons pumpkin seeds
2 tablespoons slivered almonds
2 tablespoons pine nuts
large handful coriander leaves,
    roughly chopped
large handful flat-leaf parsley leaves,
    roughly chopped
½ red onion, finely chopped
2 tablespoons salted baby capers, rinsed
½ cup (75 g) currants
juice of 1 lemon
¼ cup (60 ml) extra virgin olive oil
sea salt flakes and freshly ground
    black pepper

1 Cook the freekeh in a saucepan of simmering water for 45 minutes or until just cooked. Drain well in a colander, rinse under cold running water and leave to cool. At the same time, cook the lentils in a separate saucepan of simmering water for 20 minutes or until just tender. Drain and rinse under cold running water, then set aside.

2 Meanwhile, heat the cumin seeds in a small, dry non-stick frying pan over low–medium heat for 1–2 minutes or until they smell fragrant and are lightly toasted. Remove the cumin seeds and grind with a mortar and pestle.

3 Mix the yoghurt, honey and cumin until combined. Cover with plastic film and set aside in the fridge.

4 Put the pumpkin seeds, almonds and pine nuts into a non-stick frying pan and cook over low heat for 2 minutes or until they are lightly toasted. Remove from the pan and set aside.

5 Place the pumpkin seeds, almonds, pine nuts, coriander, parsley, onion, capers, currants, lemon juice, olive oil, freekeh and lentils in a large bowl, then season to taste with salt and pepper and mix well. Transfer to a serving bowl and serve with the cumin yoghurt.

Asparagus baked in salt crust with vinegar mayonnaise

Make sure you don't let the asparagus sit in the salt crust for any length of time before baking or it will take on too much of the salt flavour. If you are pressed for time, simply roast the asparagus with olive oil, sea salt and thyme and serve it with the vinegar mayonnaise.

225 g table salt
75 g rock salt
335 g plain flour
2 egg whites
200 ml water
12 asparagus spears, woody
    ends trimmed
sea salt flakes

VINEGAR MAYONNAISE
2 golden shallots, finely chopped
200 ml champagne vinegar
1 stem thyme
1 small clove garlic, sliced
1 fresh bay leaf
2 teaspoons caster sugar
2 teaspoons dijon mustard
3 egg yolks, at room temperature
200 ml extra virgin olive oil

1 For the vinegar mayonnaise, put the shallot, vinegar, thyme, garlic, bay leaf and sugar into a small saucepan and bring to a simmer, then cook over medium–high heat for 15 minutes or until reduced to 2 tablespoons. Set aside to cool. Strain the mixture, discarding the solids, then transfer to a bowl. Add mustard and egg yolks and whisk well. Slowly add the olive oil, drop by drop at first and then in a thin, steady stream, until the mixture emulsifies to form a mayonnaise. (Makes about 310 ml. Store any leftovers in an airtight container in the fridge for up to 3 days.)

2 For the salt crust, combine the salts and flour in a mixing bowl. Add the egg whites and water and mix until a dough forms. Wrap in plastic film, then refrigerate for 30 minutes.

3 Meanwhile, preheat the oven to 200°C fan-forced (220°C conventional).

4 Roll out the dough to 4 mm-thick and cut into two 25 cm squares. Place half of the asparagus on one side of each piece of dough and roll the dough around the asparagus to form a parcel. (Make sure there are no holes when sealing the dough around the asparagus.) Trim the edges. Put the asparagus parcels onto a baking tray lined with baking paper. Bake for 15 minutes. Remove from the oven, then immediately cut around the top of the salt crust to create a lid. Remove the salt crust lid from each parcel.

5 Season the asparagus with salt flakes, if desired, and serve with vinegar mayonnaise to the side.

MAINS

Best-ever spaghetti bolognese

This has to be one of the most frequently eaten dishes at the Australian dinner table. Make sure the boiling water for the pasta is as salty as the sea, and be careful not to overcook the spaghetti – it should still have some bite and texture. My version of this famous sauce has seventeen ingredients. Cinnamon and nutmeg are the (now not so) secret ingredients.

¼ cup (60 ml) olive oil
2 onions, finely chopped
2 carrots, finely chopped
2 sticks celery, finely chopped
3 cloves garlic, crushed
4 bay leaves
1 teaspoon cloves
300 g minced beef
300 g minced pork
300 g minced veal
2 cups (500 ml) dry white wine
1 teaspoon ground nutmeg
1 teaspoon ground cinnamon
1 × 400 g tin crushed tomato
200 g tomato paste (puree)
sea salt flakes and freshly ground
    white pepper
400 g spaghetti
shaved parmesan and oregano
    sprigs (optional), to serve

1 Heat the olive oil in a large deep saucepan over medium–high heat and cook the onion, carrot and celery for 5 minutes or until softened and coloured. Add the garlic, bay leaves and cloves and cook for another 1–2 minutes, stirring with a wooden spoon. Add the minced beef, pork and veal. Cook for 6 minutes or until browned, using a wooden spoon to break up any lumps. Add the wine, nutmeg, cinnamon, tomato and tomato paste and bring to the boil.

2 Reduce the heat to low, cover with a lid and simmer for 30 minutes; the sauce should have reduced and be rich. Season to taste with salt and pepper. Remove and discard the cloves.

3 When the sauce is ready, cook the spaghetti in a large saucepan of salted boiling water following packet instructions until al dente. Drain, then serve with the bolognese sauce, topped with shaved parmesan and scattered with oregano, if you like.

Pastitsio

My Italian friends and I often argue about what's better, lasagne or pastitsio. I have come to the conclusion that I love them both equally.

250 g dried Greek macaroni (available from Greek delicatessens or use penne)
table salt
olive oil, for drizzling

MEAT SAUCE

olive oil, for cooking
1 onion, finely chopped
2 cloves garlic, sliced
1 tablespoon finely chopped thyme
300 g minced lamb
100 g minced veal
100 g minced pork
2 tablespoons tomato paste (puree)
1 × 400 g tin crushed tomato
1 stick cinnamon
sea salt flakes

BECHAMEL SAUCE WITH PARMESAN

100 g unsalted butter, chopped
⅔ cup (100 g) plain flour
400 ml milk
400 ml thickened cream
3 eggs, beaten
200 g parmesan, grated
sea salt flakes and freshly ground white pepper

1 For the meat sauce, heat 1 tablespoon olive oil in a frying pan over medium heat. Cook the onion, garlic and thyme for 3 minutes or until soft, then add the minced lamb, veal and pork. Cook for 5 minutes or until browned, using a wooden spoon to break up any lumps. Add the tomato paste, tomato and cinnamon, then reduce the heat to low, cover with a lid and simmer for 30 minutes. Season to taste with salt and set aside.

2 For the bechamel sauce, melt the butter in a saucepan over low heat. Add the flour, then stir for 2 minutes or until you have a smooth paste. Slowly add the milk and cream, continuing to stir until the sauce is smooth and thick; this can take up to 15 minutes. Remove the pan from the heat and cover with a lid. Leave to cool for 10 minutes. Stir in the beaten egg and half of the grated parmesan. Season to taste with salt and pepper. Set aside.

3 Meanwhile, cook the pasta in a saucepan of boiling salted water following packet instructions until al dente, then drain and toss with a splash of olive oil. Spread out on a baking tray and leave to cool.

4 Preheat the oven to 180°C fan-forced (200°C conventional). Lightly oil a 30 × 20 cm baking dish.

5 Arrange the pasta on the base of the dish, then scatter over the remaining parmesan. Cover with a little of the bechamel, then top with the meat sauce and finish with a thick layer of bechamel. Bake the pastitsio for 30–40 minutes or until the top is golden brown. Leave for 20 minutes before cutting and serving.

Haloumi and mint ravioli with burnt butter and raisins

I borrowed the idea for this recipe from my mum, who would cook the ravioli in chicken broth and serve it in the broth finished with egg and lemon. My version is a lot richer than hers as I've topped the pasta with melted butter. She probably wouldn't eat it – she'd ask why I've used so much butter!

400 g haloumi cheese (see page 141)
200 g firm ricotta, drained
3 eggs, 1 lightly beaten
10 mint leaves, finely shredded, plus
    extra leaves to serve
1 quantity Pasta Dough (see page 135)
fine semolina, for dusting
table salt
150 g unsalted butter, chopped
130 g raisins
130 g pistachios, toasted, peeled

1 Preheat the oven to 190°C fan-forced (210°C conventional).

2 Bake the haloumi on a baking tray for 20 minutes or until golden brown. Cool in the fridge. Finely grate the haloumi into a mixing bowl. Add the ricotta, the 2 unbeaten eggs and the shredded mint. Mix well, then divide into 12 balls. Set aside.

3 Make and roll the pasta following the instructions on page 135. On a bench dusted with semolina, take a sheet of pasta and put 6 balls of haloumi mixture in a row down the centre, at 10 cm intervals. Lightly brush in between the filling with beaten egg. Place another pasta sheet on top, press around the filling to remove any air bubbles, then cut into 6 cm squares (if you want round ravioli, then cut them with a 6 cm pastry cutter). Place the ravioli on a baking tray dusted with semolina. Repeat with the remaining pasta sheets and filling.

4 Cook the ravioli in a saucepan of boiling salted water for 4 minutes or until they float to the surface. Remove with a slotted spoon and place in warm serving bowls. Meanwhile, melt the butter in a frying pan over high heat until it turns light brown, then add the raisins and pistachios and pour this over the ravioli immediately. Scatter with extra mint leaves and serve at once.

Prawn risotto

Everyone has their own idea of how to make risotto, but the key to my recipe is to not stir the rice while adding the stock. That way, the starch in the rice doesn't make the risotto claggy – I like to see all the grains of rice loose and separate. Instead of making stock from the prawn shells, you could use the same quantity of fish stock.

40 g unsalted butter
1 tablespoon olive oil
1 onion, finely chopped
2 cloves garlic, crushed
1 cup (200 g) carnaroli rice
    (see page 140)
12 raw king prawns, peeled,
    cleaned and sliced, shells
    reserved for making stock
mascarpone and chervil sprigs
    (optional), to serve
sea salt flakes and freshly ground
    black pepper

PRAWN STOCK
reserved shells from the peeled
    prawns (see above)
1 tablespoon olive oil
1 cup (250 ml) dry white wine
1 tablespoon tomato paste (puree)
2 cloves garlic, roughly chopped
2 golden shallots, roughly chopped
1 litre water

1 For the prawn stock, put the prawn shells into a heavy-based saucepan and drizzle with the olive oil. Cook over medium heat for 15 minutes, stirring. Remove the pan from the heat and deglaze with the wine, stirring to remove any bits stuck to the base of the pan. Return the pan to medium heat, then add the tomato paste, garlic, shallot and water. Bring to the boil, then reduce the heat to low and simmer for 25 minutes. Strain the stock through a fine-mesh sieve into a saucepan and discard the solids. Keep the stock warm.

2 Heat half of the butter with the olive oil in a large heavy-based saucepan over medium–high heat. Add the onion and garlic and cook for 2 minutes or until soft. Add the rice and continue to stir for 2 minutes or until it is translucent and lightly toasted. Add 3 cups (750 ml) of the hot prawn stock, reduce the heat to low, then simmer gently for 12–14 minutes until all the liquid has been absorbed.

3 When the rice is tender to the bite, but ever so slightly firm in the centre (al dente), remove the pan from the heat and add the prawns and remaining butter. (The prawns should gently cook in the residual heat of the pan off the heat.) Mix well to achieve a creamy consistency and adjust the risotto by adding an extra ½ cup (125 ml) of the warm stock, if you want it to be a bit looser. Check that the prawns are cooked (if not, continue to stir until the prawns are just cookedthrough).

4 Divide the risotto among plates or bowls, top with a spoonful of mascarpone (if using), then season with salt and pepper and scatter with chervil, if you like. Serve immediately.

Braised chicken and celery fricassee

I use chicken marylands for this recipe as I think the dark meat has much more flavour and is juicier than the breast. It's very Greek to finish a dish with egg and lemon – and you know why? The flavours are great!

¼ cup (60 ml) olive oil
4 chicken marylands (leg and thigh portions)
sea salt flakes
6 sticks celery, thinly sliced
1 onion, diced
3 cloves garlic, finely chopped
2 teaspoons dried oregano
3 stems thyme
1.5 litres Chicken Stock (see page 134)
1 iceberg lettuce, trimmed, cut into
    3 cm squares
large handful dill, finely chopped
100 ml lemon juice
4 eggs
dill sprigs and garlic chive buds (optional),
    to serve

1 Preheat the oven to 160°C fan-forced (180°C conventional).

2 Heat the olive oil in a heavy-based frying pan over medium heat and cook the chicken pieces, turning until golden brown on both sides, for 5 minutes. Transfer the chicken to a flameproof roasting pan and season well with salt.

3 Add the celery, onion, garlic and oregano to the frying pan and cook over medium heat for 4–5 minutes. Spoon over the chicken pieces, along with the thyme, then add the chicken stock. Cover tightly with foil and bake for 1¼–1½ hours or until the chicken is tender.

4 Remove the chicken pieces from the roasting pan, then put the pan over medium heat, bring the liquid to the boil and simmer until reduced by half. Add the lettuce, dill and lemon juice to the reduced sauce.

5 Whisk the eggs in a bowl until light and foamy. Add ½ cup (125 ml) of the hot stock and whisk to combine well, then pour the egg mixture into the pan. Stir over low heat for 2–3 minutes or until the mixture thickens slightly; do not boil or the mixture will curdle. Season to taste with salt. Return the chicken to the pan to warm through. Serve immediately, scattered with herbs, if desired, with the remaining sauce in a jug on the table.

Chicken and sweetcorn pie

To make a quick version of this comforting pie, simply fill individual ramekins with the chicken filling, then top with rounds of ready-made puff pastry and bake until golden.

25 g unsalted butter
1 kg skinless chicken thigh fillets, cut
    into 2 cm pieces
2 leeks, white part only, well washed,
    thinly sliced
1 clove garlic, finely chopped
4 stems thyme
¼ cup (35 g) plain flour
1 cup (250 ml) Chicken Stock
    (see page 134)
1½ cups (240 g) corn kernels
4 tablespoons chopped flat-leaf parsley
sea salt flakes and freshly ground
    black pepper
1 quantity Maggie Beer's Sour-cream
    Pastry (see page 137)
1 egg, beaten
1 sheet frozen butter puff pastry, thawed

1 Melt the butter in a large frying pan over medium heat. Cook the chicken in batches for 2–3 minutes on each side. Remove from the pan and set aside. Add the leek to the pan and cook over low heat for 2–3 minutes. Stir in the garlic and thyme. Sprinkle in the flour, stirring well to combine, then add the stock and bring to a gentle simmer. Cook for 2–3 minutes, stirring constantly so there are no lumps. Return the chicken to the pan and simmer for 4–5 minutes or until cooked through. Add the corn and parsley, then season to taste with salt and pepper and mix well. Remove from the heat and refrigerate until completely cold.

2 On a bench dusted with flour, roll out the sour-cream pastry to 5 mm thick. Use the pastry to line the base and sides of a 1 litre-capacity baking dish, then trim around the edge with a sharp knife. Patch any tears and holes with the pastry off-cuts. Spoon the cooled filling into the dish. Wet the edges of the pastry base with some of the beaten egg, then gently lay the puff pastry over the top of the pie filling and trim around the edge, allowing a little overhang. Press the edges together with a fork and brush with beaten egg. Cut a small cross in the top of the pie with a small, sharp knife to enable steam to escape (this helps the pastry to rise, so it doesn't get soggy). Refrigerate the pie for 30 minutes.

3 Preheat the oven to 200°C fan-forced (220°C conventional).

4 Brush the pastry with beaten egg one last time. Bake the pie for 40 minutes or until golden brown. Serve slices of the pie hot, warm or cold.

Chicken braised with potato, tomatoes and cinnamon

SERVES 4–6

Matching chicken with cinnamon might sound odd, but in traditional Greek cooking it is very common to use cinnamon in savoury dishes. I even add a little to my spaghetti bolognese (see page 54).

1 teaspoon cumin seeds
1 teaspoon coriander seeds
100 ml olive oil
4 chicken marylands (leg and thigh portions, about 1.2 kg), thighs and drumsticks separated
2 onions, thinly sliced
2 cloves garlic, finely chopped
1 stick cinnamon
3 nicola potatoes (about 600 g), thinly sliced
finely grated zest of 1 lemon
sea salt flakes
200 ml Chicken Stock (see page 134)
500 g cherry tomatoes
freshly ground black pepper
flat-leaf parsley, to garnish

1 Preheat the oven to 180°C fan-forced (200°C conventional).

2 Heat the cumin and coriander seeds in a small, dry non-stick frying pan over low–medium heat for 1–2 minutes or until fragrant and lightly toasted. Crush with a mortar and pestle until finely ground. Set aside.

3 Heat the olive oil in a large heavy-based frying pan over high heat, then add the chicken and cook for 5 minutes on each side or until browned. Remove and set aside. Add the onion, garlic, cinnamon and ground spices to the pan. Reduce the heat to medium and cook for 5 minutes, stirring until the onion is soft. Add the potato and cook for a further 5 minutes.

4 Spread the potato slices over the base of a baking dish large enough to hold the chicken in a single layer (my dish is 36 cm × 24 cm). Place the browned chicken, skin-side up, over the potato, then scatter over the onion mixture and lemon zest and season with a little salt.

5 Add the stock and tomatoes, then cover with foil and roast for 45 minutes. Remove the foil and continue to roast for another 20 minutes or until the chicken is golden and cooked through. Season to taste with pepper. Scatter with parsley and serve.

Quails wrapped in vine leaves

This quail dish is inspired by traditional dolmades. That's what's so exciting about food – one idea often leads to another.

4 quails
2 tablespoons rosemary, finely chopped
125 g unsalted butter, softened
sea salt flakes and freshly ground black pepper
8 preserved vine leaves
olive oil, for cooking

1 To butterfly the quails, use kitchen scissors to cut out the backbone. Next, cut through the breast bone. You will have 2 halves. Use your fingers to remove the small ribcage bones. Use the kitchen scissors to cut off the wings, then discard. Pat the quails dry with paper towel and set aside.

2 Mix the rosemary and butter in a small bowl until combined. Season to taste with salt and pepper and set aside.

3 Rinse the vine leaves under cold running water, then pat dry with paper towel. Lay the vine leaves on a chopping board.

4 Lay 1 quail half in the middle of each vine leaf, skin-side down, then spread 1 teaspoonful of rosemary butter over the flesh. Wrap each quail half in a vine leaf so a leg bone sticks out the end (as in the photo here).

5 Preheat the oven to 180°C fan-forced (200°C conventional).

6 Heat a heavy-based frying pan over medium heat, then add 1 tablespoon of the olive oil and fry 2 of the wrapped quail halves for 1 minute on each side to seal. Repeat with the remaining quail halves, adding more oil to the pan if necessary.

7 Wrap each quail half in foil. Transfer to a baking tray and bake for 4–5 minutes; the quails should be cooked through. Remove the quail parcels from the oven, discard the foil and serve.

Rabbit stifado

I have childhood memories of friends coming to my house, taking one look at the big pot of stifado on the stove and saying, 'Ugh! You can't eat rabbit! No-one eats rabbit!' Well, rabbit is one of the most delicious meats, and is especially flavoursome when cooked in this classic Greek stew with loads of onion that turns sweet as the pot simmers.

1 × 1.5 kg rabbit, jointed (ask your butcher
    to do this)
½ cup (125 ml) extra virgin olive oil
1 fresh bay leaf
3 stems thyme
1 head garlic, cloves separated, gently bruised
    with the side of a knife
2 onions, halved, thinly sliced
100 ml samos vin doux sweet wine (see page 141)
    or sauternes
2 cups (500 ml) Chicken Stock (see page 134)
100 g natural Greek-style yoghurt
honey (optional), to taste
sea salt flakes and freshly ground white pepper

1 Preheat the oven to 160°C fan-forced (180°C conventional).

2 Place the rabbit, ¼ cup (60 ml) of the olive oil, the bay leaf, thyme and garlic in a bowl and toss to coat the rabbit in oil. Cover with plastic film and refrigerate for 30 minutes.

3 Meanwhile, heat the remaining olive oil in a deep ovenproof frying pan or enamelled cast-iron casserole over low–medium heat. Add the onion and cook for 20 minutes or until translucent, stirring occasionally. Transfer the onion to a bowl with a slotted spoon and set aside.

4 Return the pan to medium heat. Add the rabbit pieces and cook for 1 minute on each side or until light golden. Add the bay leaf, thyme, garlic and remaining oil from the bowl and return the onion to the pan. Stir in the wine and stock. Cover with a piece of baking paper (cartouche, see page 140), then a tight-fitting lid. Transfer to the oven to cook for 45 minutes. If the meat on the forelegs is cooked through and tender, remove it now, then continue to cook the remaining rabbit pieces for a further 15 minutes or until the hind legs are tender and the meat pulls easily away from the bone.

5 Transfer the rabbit pieces to a clean bowl. Put the pan over medium heat and reduce the sauce by one-third. Reduce the heat to low and stir in the yoghurt, then add honey to taste (if using). Season to taste with salt and pepper. Remove and discard the bay leaf and thyme, if desired. Serve the rabbit with the sauce spooned over.

Slow-roasted pork belly
with compressed apple

This dish is perfect for a dinner party – it's a real conversation stopper when it arrives at the table. Compressing the apple in ziplock bags with citric acid preserves it and stops it from going brown. Citric acid occurs naturally in citrus fruits and is used mainly to add a tangy sour flavour. When buying pork belly, ask the butcher for the thicker end, as this will cook more evenly and will stay beautifully moist.

1 × 1.5 kg piece pork belly, bones removed, skin scored (ask your butcher to do this)
2 tablespoons ground cinnamon
1 tablespoon ground star anise
2 tablespoons sea salt flakes
2 tablespoons olive oil
freshly ground black pepper
thyme flowers (optional), to serve

COMPRESSED APPLE
4 granny smith apples
2 tablespoons caster sugar
2 teaspoons citric acid (see page 140)

1 Preheat the oven to 120°C fan-forced (140°C conventional).

2 Put the pork belly onto a chopping board. Mix the cinnamon, star anise and salt in a small bowl and rub all over the pork belly. Drizzle a large roasting pan with olive oil. Put the pork belly into the pan, skin-side down, then drizzle with a little more olive oil. Roast the pork belly for 2½ hours. Carefully turn the pork belly over so the skin-side is facing up.

3 Meanwhile, for the compressed apple, peel the apples and slice widthways into 1 cm-thick rounds. Mix the sugar and citric acid in a small bowl, then sprinkle over the apple slices. Place each re-formed apple in a ziplock bag and squeeze out the air. Refrigerate for at least 2 hours.

4 Increase the oven temperature to 170°C fan-forced (190°C conventional) and roast the pork for another 30 minutes or until the skin is crisp and crunchy.

5 Remove the pork belly from the oven. (Do not cover as this softens the crackling.) Set aside to rest for 15 minutes.

6 Remove the apple from the ziplock bags. Slice the pork belly, scatter with thyme flowers (if using), season with salt and serve with the compressed apple.

Lamb on a spit

The ritual of cooking lamb on a spit is about celebrating and eating the whole beast, not just the sweet cuts. In the restaurant we marinate the lamb in the cool room. If you decide to give spit-roasting a go, order a whole lamb in advance from a Greek or Middle Eastern butcher and borrow or hire a spit-roast rotisserie. You will need a clean garbage bag large enough to accommodate the marinating lamb and enough ice to fill your bathtub to keep the lamb cold as it marinates overnight.

1 × 12 kg whole lamb (available from Greek
   and Middle Eastern butchers)
8 stems dried Greek oregano (rigani),
   leaves only (to yield 6 tablespoons)
4 onions, roughly chopped
4 cloves garlic, peeled
1 cup (250 ml) extra virgin olive oil
sea salt flakes and freshly ground
   black pepper
plenty of ice

1 Wipe the lamb inside and out with paper towel.

2 Combine the oregano, onion, garlic and olive oil in a bowl, then season with loads of salt and pepper. Rub the mixture all over the inside cavity and exterior of the lamb. Place the lamb in a clean large garbage bag and seal. Leave to marinate in the fridge or a clean ice-filled bathtub overnight.

3 Remove the lamb from the fridge or bathtub. Leave to come to room temperature.

4 An hour before you wish to start cooking the lamb, have a fire ready in the hearth of a rotating spit appliance set up in a safe place outside (follow the manufacturer's instructions). Use a combination of wood and coal or barbecue heat beads and burn until the coal or heat beads are glowing white, about 45–60 minutes.

5 Remove the lamb from the garbage bag and secure it onto the spit, following the manufacturer's instructions. Cook the lamb for 3–4 hours or until the meat is tender, basting it frequently with any remaining marinade during cooking. Add a handful of extra coals or heat beads to the fire every 10 minutes to maintain the heat. (The cooking time can vary considerably, depending on the outside temperature and the wind.)

6 Remove the lamb from the spit and carve it into chunks, then place on a large platter and serve. (Or do what my family does and eat it hot, straight from the spit!)

Keftedes

Keftedes are the Greek version of meatballs. Leftovers taste especially good slipped into a white bread sandwich along with your favourite pickles.

**3 slices stale white bread with crusts
(75 g), torn**
1 cup (250 ml) milk
500 g minced lamb
1 onion, finely chopped
2 cloves garlic, finely chopped
1 tablespoon finely chopped oregano
1 tablespoon finely chopped mint
**3 tablespoons finely chopped
flat-leaf parsley**
2 teaspoons white-wine vinegar
1 egg, beaten
¼ teaspoon freshly grated nutmeg
sea salt flakes
⅓ cup (50 g) plain flour, for coating
olive oil, for shallow-frying
**natural Greek-style yoghurt and
lemon wedges, to serve**
green salad (optional), to serve

1 Soak the bread in the milk for 5 minutes, then squeeze out excess milk and put the bread into a large bowl. (Discard the leftover milk.) Add the minced lamb, onion, garlic, oregano, mint, parsley, vinegar, egg and nutmeg to the bowl, then season with salt and mix with your hands, squeezing well to combine all the ingredients. Cover with plastic film and refrigerate for 30 minutes to allow the flavours to develop.

2 Roll the lamb mixture into elongated meatballs; you should have about 24. Roll in flour to coat.

3 Pour enough olive oil for shallow-frying into a heavy-based frying pan. Heat over medium heat, then cook the meatballs in batches for 3 minutes on each side or until cooked through and browned.

4 Remove the meatballs from the pan and drain on paper towel. Serve the keftedes on a plate with lemon wedges and a bowl of yoghurt with salad to the side, if desired.

Mum's slow-cooked lamb

As a kid, I would sometimes complain about my mum's cooking but now I can't get enough of it. This childhood favourite is so good and the leftovers taste even better the next day.

¼ cup (60 ml) olive oil
8 large outer sticks celery, cut into
    5 cm lengths
8 lamb chump chops
1 tablespoon coriander seeds
1 tablespoon cumin seeds
2 sticks cinnamon
1 × 400 g tin crushed tomato
2 cups (500 ml) water
sea salt flakes and freshly ground
    white pepper
flat-leaf parsley, to serve

1 Preheat the oven to 140°C fan-forced (160°C conventional).

2 Drizzle half of the olive oil over the base of a large roasting pan or baking dish. Put the celery and lamb chops into the dish. Scatter over the coriander, cumin, cinnamon and tomato, then add the water. Season with salt and pepper and cover tightly with foil.

3 Bake the lamb for 3 hours or until tender. Remove the foil and bake for a further 20 minutes to brown the lamb. Remove the pan from the oven, drizzle with the remaining olive oil and scatter with parsley. Serve.

Braised lamb shanks

If you don't have a pressure cooker, I encourage you to invest in one. Once you've nailed the technique for using a pressure cooker, you'll be ripping out some of the best dishes and saving yourself loads of time in the process. A pressure cooker also vacuum-seals the flavour into whatever you're cooking, so what's not to love! Alternatively, simply braise the lamb in an enamelled cast-iron casserole in a 160°C fan-forced (180°C conventional) oven for 2 hours or until meltingly tender.

1 tablespoon coriander seeds
sea salt flakes
2 tablespoons plain flour, for dusting
6 lamb shanks, French-trimmed (excess
    fat and sinew removed)
2 tablespoons olive oil
6 golden shallots, finely chopped
3 cloves garlic, finely chopped
1 cup (250 ml) dry white wine
2 long stems rosemary
1 stick cinnamon
1 fresh bay leaf
6 white peppercorns
zest of ½ orange, in strips, white
    pith removed
1.2 litres Chicken Stock (see page 134)
about 1 cup (250 ml) water

1 Heat the coriander seeds in a small, dry non-stick frying pan over low–medium heat for 1–2 minutes or until fragrant and lightly toasted. Using a mortar and pestle, grind the coriander seeds with 1 teaspoon salt until finely ground. Combine the coriander and salt mixture with the flour in a bowl. Dust each lamb shank in this mixture to coat well, shaking to remove any excess.

2 Heat the olive oil in a large non-stick frying pan over medium–high heat. Working in batches, cook the lamb shanks for 5 minutes, turning occasionally until well browned all over. Transfer to a pressure cooker. Return the frying pan to low–medium heat, then saute the shallot until softened, approximately 3 minutes. Stir in the garlic and the wine, then bring to the boil over high heat, scraping well to remove any caught bits stuck to the base of the pan.

3 Transfer the shallot, garlic and wine mixture to the pressure cooker. Add the rosemary, cinnamon, bay leaf, peppercorns, orange zest and stock. Pour in enough water to just cover the shanks, then secure on the lid.

4 Put the pressure cooker over high heat and bring to low pressure. Reduce the heat to low to maintain a gentle release of steam (follow the manufacturer's instructions) and cook for 25 minutes. (The steam should make a low constant hissing sound.) Turn off the heat and release the steam (follow the manufacturer's instructions), then carefully remove the lid.

5 Transfer the shanks to a bowl, then cover with foil to keep warm. Remove the cinnamon stick. Place the pressure cooker over high heat and bring the liquid to the boil. Simmer until it has reduced by two-thirds and is a sauce consistency, approximately 20 minutes.

6 Serve the shanks with the sauce spooned over.

Veal shanks with mastic and yoghurt

This dish needs time – low temperatures and long cooking are the secrets to its success. You should be able to eat the meat with a fork, no knife required! What's especially delicious is how the yoghurt turns into a squeaky, tasty cheese when cooked in this way. You don't have to use mastic but it adds a unique flavour.

¼ cup (80 ml) olive oil
4 veal shanks (about 650 g each)
6 pearl onions, peeled
6 golden shallots, peeled
1 red onion, roughly chopped
2 onions, roughly chopped
1 leek, white part only, well washed,
    cut into 2 cm pieces
5 drops mastic oil or 1 mastic bead
    (see page 141), ground
6 cloves garlic, peeled
6 stems thyme
200 ml dry white wine
finely grated zest of 2 lemons
50 g honey
about 1.2 litres Chicken Stock (see
    page 134)
500 g natural Greek-style yoghurt
micro herbs and red perilla leaves
    (optional), to serve

1 Preheat the oven to 120°C fan-forced (140°C conventional).

2 Heat the olive oil in a heavy-based frying pan over medium–high heat, then add the veal shanks and cook, turning, for 7 minutes or until dark and caramelised. Transfer to a deep roasting pan. Add the pearl onions, shallots, red and brown onions, leek, mastic, garlic, thyme, wine and lemon zest to the roasting pan. Drizzle over the honey and add enough chicken stock to almost, but not quite, cover the veal and vegetables; do not add too much stock to the pan.

3 Spread the yoghurt over the veal, vegetables and stock, then top with a sheet of baking paper (cartouche, see page 140). Cover the pan with foil and seal tightly. Bake for 6½–7 hours or until the veal is tender. Remove from the oven and set aside.

4 Remove the veal shanks and yoghurt 'cheese' from the roasting pan and keep warm. Strain the liquid through a fine-mesh sieve into a saucepan, discarding the solids. Simmer over low–medium heat until reduced by three-quarters to make a sauce sauce. Pour the sauce over the veal. Serve the veal shanks topped with the yoghurt 'cheese' and herbs, if desired.

Twice-cooked lamb ribs

Cooking the ribs twice makes them crisp on the outside and succulent in the centre. I love the flavour of pumpkin seeds with savoury food (and sweet food too).

1 tablespoon coriander seeds
2 teaspoons cumin seeds
1 kg lamb ribs (about 24 ribs), trimmed
    of excess fat, cut into sections
    of 4–6 ribs
1 litre Chicken Stock (see page 134)
    or water
1 cup (250 ml) white wine
1 onion, roughly chopped
3 cloves garlic, halved
3 stems rosemary
1 star anise
6 black peppercorns
table salt
vegetable oil, for shallow-frying
natural Greek-style yoghurt, extra
    virgin olive oil, toasted pumpkin
    seeds and mint sprigs, to serve

SPICE COATING
4 tablespoons coriander seeds
3 tablespoons cumin seeds
1 tablespoon smoked paprika (see page 141)
½ teaspoon cayenne
1 cup (150 g) plain flour
sea salt flakes

1 Heat the coriander seeds and cumin seeds in a small dry frying pan over low–medium heat for 1–2 minutes or until fragrant and lightly toasted. Lightly crush with a mortar and pestle. Set aside.

2 Put the ribs, stock or water, wine, onion, garlic, rosemary, star anise, peppercorns, crushed coriander seeds and cumin seeds and 1 teaspoon salt into a large saucepan. Add more water if necessary to cover the ribs. Bring to the boil over high heat, skimming off any scum that rises to the surface. Reduce the heat to low, cover with the lid and simmer gently for 1½ hours or until the meat easily pulls away from the bones. Set the ribs aside in the cooking liquid until completely cooled. (The ribs and stock can be covered and refrigerated at this point for up to 4 days.)

3 Remove the ribs from the stock and dry with paper towel. Slice between each bone to cut the racks into single ribs. Discard the cooking liquid.

4 For the spice coating, heat the coriander seeds and cumin seeds in a small dry non-stick frying pan over low–medium heat for 1–2 minutes or until fragrant and lightly toasted. Lightly crush with a mortar and pestle. Combine the ground spices, paprika, cayenne, flour and 2 teaspoons salt in a wide, shallow bowl. Working with 4–6 ribs at a time, toss the ribs in the spice coating to coat well and shake off excess. Repeat with the remaining ribs and spice coating.

5 Meanwhile, heat enough oil for shallow-frying (about 1 cm) in a frying pan over medium–high heat. Fry 6 ribs at a time for 1–2 minutes on each side or until golden and crisp. Drain on paper towel. Repeat with the remaining ribs.

6 Transfer the ribs to a platter. Dollop with yoghurt, drizzle with olive oil and scatter with pumpkin seeds and mint sprigs. Season with salt. Serve.

Pan-fried john dory with almonds

This recipe is based on the classic French dish sole meunière. It is a beautiful thing to melt butter to the point where it turns nut-brown and then tip it over perfectly cooked sweet white fish, such as john dory.

50 g whole blanched almonds
4 × 450 g john dory, scaled, cleaned
sea salt flakes and freshly ground
    white pepper
¼ cup (60 ml) olive oil
80 g unsalted butter, chopped
2 tablespoons salted capers, rinsed
2 tablespoons roughly chopped
    flat-leaf parsley
juice of 1 lemon
baby cos lettuce leaves (optional),
    to serve

1 Preheat the oven to 175°C fan-forced (195°C conventional).

2 Spread the almonds on a baking tray and roast for 8 minutes or until golden. Set aside.

3 Working with one fish at a time, cut off the tail, head and gills. (Keep the head and tail for making stock, if desired.) Trim away the flap of flesh around the belly on each side of the fish. Using kitchen scissors, trim and remove the fins.

4 To remove the skin, place each fish skin-side down on a chopping board. Using a sharp, flexible filleting knife, start sliding the blade from the tail-end, working the blade along between the skin and flesh while gripping onto the skin with the other hand. Continue this sliding and slicing motion along the length of the fish to separate the skin and discard. Repeat to remove the skin from the other side.

5 Wipe the fish dry with paper towel. Season with a little salt and pepper.

6 Heat the olive oil in a large ovenproof non-stick frying pan over high heat. Add all 4 fish and cook for 3 minutes or until nicely browned on one side. Carefully loosen each fish from the base of the pan with a spatula and turn over. Transfer the pan to the oven and roast for 4 minutes or until the fish are just cooked through. Transfer the fish to 4 warmed serving plates and set aside.

7 Working quickly, wipe the pan clean with paper towel and return to medium–high heat. Add the butter and, when it begins to sizzle, add the almonds, capers and parsley and toss for 1 minute, then stir in the lemon juice. Remove immediately from the heat and spoon the almonds, capers, parsley and buttery pan juices over the fish.

8 Scatter with baby cos leaves (if using) and serve immediately.

Millionaire's moussaka

I named this dish 'millionaires' moussaka' as it has
a number of extravagant ingredients – namely
lobster and caviar. You don't have to be a millionaire
to make or eat it – you just have to love food.
Use prawns instead of lobster if you prefer.

2 bulbs baby fennel, trimmed, tops reserved,
    bulbs cut into eighths
2 tablespoons olive oil
sea salt flakes
1 × 750 g live lobster, put into the freezer for 1 hour
1 carrot, cut into 3 cm pieces
1 onion, cut into 3 cm pieces
2 sticks celery, cut into 3 cm pieces
2 fresh bay leaves
1 lemon, halved
1 orange, halved
ice cubes
2 eggs
6 small kipfler potatoes
caviar (optional), to serve

BECHAMEL SAUCE WITH KEFALOGRAVIERA
300 ml milk
3 stems thyme
½ clove garlic, bruised
1 wedge onion, sliced
30 g unsalted butter
30 g plain flour
20 g kefalograviera cheese (see page 141)

1 Preheat the oven to 180°C fan-forced
(200°C conventional).

2 Put the fennel into a roasting pan, pour over the
olive oil and season with salt. Roast for 30 minutes
or until tender, turning halfway through cooking.
Remove and set aside.

3 Put the lobster onto a chopping board, then
insert the tip of a sharp, heavy-bladed knife into
the centre of its head. Using a strong, single
movement, push the knife down onto the board,
along the front of the head, splitting the lobster
in 2 lengthways along the mid-line. Remove
and discard the shell and central vein, then cut
the flesh into 5 mm-thick slices. Set aside.

4 Fill a large saucepan just over three-quarters full
of water, then add the carrot, onion, celery, bay
leaves, lemon, orange and reserved fennel tops.
Bring to the boil and cook for 5 minutes. Add the
lobster to the pan and cook for 6 minutes. Transfer
the lobster to a sink or bucket full of iced water;
this stops it from cooking further. Leave in the iced
water for 5 minutes, then remove and refrigerate.
Discard the vegetables and aromatics.

5 Put the eggs into a small saucepan. Cover with
cold water and bring to the boil over high heat.
Reduce the heat to medium, then cook for
3 minutes. Drain, then refresh in iced water.
Peel and cut into 1 cm-thick slices. Set aside.

6 Put the potatoes into a saucepan of cold water
and bring to a simmer over high heat, then cook
for 10 minutes or until tender. Drain, then slice.

7 For the bechamel sauce, put the milk, thyme,
garlic and onion into a saucepan. Heat over very
low heat until close to simmering, then remove from
the heat and leave to infuse for 30 minutes. Heat
the butter in a heavy-based saucepan over medium
heat until melted, then add the flour and cook for
2 minutes, stirring constantly with a wooden spoon.
Slowly add the warm milk, straining it into the pan
through a fine-mesh sieve and whisking continually
so no lumps form; discard the solids. Grate the
cheese into the sauce and mix well.

8 Preheat the oven to 170°C fan-forced
(190°C conventional).

9 Take 2 small copper or other ovenproof
saucepans (mine are 400 ml capacity), and in
each one place a layer of potato, a layer of fennel
and a layer of egg. Place 2 slices of lobster on top,
then continue this layering process until all the
potato, fennel, egg and lobster are used, finishing
with lobster. Spoon over enough bechamel sauce
to cover. (Leftover bechamel sauce can be stored
in an airtight container in the fridge for up to
3 days.) Bake until golden and heated through,
17–20 minutes. Serve the moussaka with a little
caviar spooned on top of the bechamel sauce,
if desired.

Crisp-skinned barramundi with warm chorizo, caper and anchovy vinaigrette

SERVES 4

Learning how to cook fish properly can be daunting, but once you master it, your confidence will soar. Getting it right is all about controlling the temperature. The trick to this warm vinaigrette lies in extracting the spicy flavour from the chorizo.

4 × 200 g barramundi fillets (about
    1.5 cm thick), skin-on
sea salt flakes
100 ml vegetable oil
40 g unsalted butter
1 tablespoon lemon thyme
    leaves (optional)
thinly sliced flat-leaf parsley and
    oregano sprigs, to serve

WARM CHORIZO, CAPER AND
ANCHOVY VINAIGRETTE
100 ml extra virgin olive oil
130 g good-quality chorizo, skin
    removed, coarsely crumbled into
    small pieces
2 golden shallots, thinly sliced
1 clove garlic, finely chopped
2 anchovy fillets, chopped
1 tablespoon salted capers, rinsed, drained
12 kalamata olives, pitted
sherry vinegar, to taste
3 tablespoons shredded flat-leaf parsley

1 Preheat the oven to 180°C fan-forced (200°C conventional).

2 Remove the fish from the fridge 10 minutes before cooking. Pat the fish dry with paper towel. Season the skin with salt.

3 Heat the oil in an ovenproof non-stick frying pan over medium–high heat. Place the fish in the pan, skin-side down, and gently press on each fillet with a spatula for 20–30 seconds to help the skin crisp evenly. Transfer the pan to the oven and roast the fish for 5–6 minutes or until almost cooked through.

4 Remove the fish from the oven and place the pan over medium–high heat. Working quickly, carefully turn the fish over and add the butter to the pan. When the butter starts to sizzle, add the lemon thyme (if using), then gently swirl the pan until the butter turns nut-brown and the fish is just cooked. Remove from the heat. Spoon the butter over the fish to baste several times.

5 For the vinaigrette, heat the olive oil in a non-stick frying pan over medium–high heat. Add the chorizo, then toss until the fat starts to render and the meat is browned. Using a slotted spoon, remove the chorizo and set aside. Reduce the heat to low, then add the shallot and garlic and stir until softened, 1–2 minutes. Return the chorizo to the pan. Add the anchovies, capers and olives and toss for 30 seconds. Stir in the sherry vinegar and swirl the pan, then immediately remove from the heat.

6 Put the fish, skin-side up, onto warmed plates, with the pan juices spooned over each fillet. Scatter the vinaigrette with the parsley, then spoon around each plate. Scatter with parsley and oregano sprigs and serve immediately.

Braised onion pie

This dish is my interpretation of the traditional spanakopita that Mum often made for us when we were growing up. Instead of spinach, I've made members of the onion family the heroes of this pie. The combined flavours of onion, shallot and leek are delicious with the ricotta and feta.

⅔ cup (160 ml) extra virgin olive oil
12 onions, thinly sliced
4 cloves garlic, thinly sliced
8 golden shallots, thinly sliced
3 leeks, white part only, well washed,
     thinly sliced
10 stems thyme
2 fresh bay leaves
400 g firm ricotta
400 g feta, crumbled
olive oil spray, for greasing
18 sheets filo pastry
200 ml clarified butter (see
     page 140), melted
sea salt flakes

1 Heat the olive oil in a heavy-based saucepan over medium heat and add the onion, garlic, shallot and leek, then stir for 5 minutes. Add the thyme and bay leaves, then reduce the heat to low and cook for 45 minutes or until caramelised, stirring frequently to prevent the onion from catching. Remove from the heat and set aside to cool.

2 Discard the thyme sprigs and bay leaves. Add the ricotta and feta cheese to the onion mixture and mix well.

3 Preheat the oven to 170°C fan-forced (190°C conventional).

4 Spray the base of a large roasting pan (mine is 30 × 24 cm) with olive oil spray, then line the base and sides with baking paper. Brush 1 sheet of filo pastry with clarified butter. Place in the base of the pan, trimming to fit. Repeat with 7 more sheets of filo so there are 8 layers of pastry. Place half of the onion mixture evenly over the filo. Place another 3 buttered sheets of filo pastry over the onion mixture, trim to fit, then brush with clarified butter. Place the remaining onion mixture evenly over the filo. Place another 7 buttered sheets of filo pastry on top and trim to fit again. Brush with clarified butter.

5 Bake the pie for 45 minutes or until golden brown. Sprinkle with salt and serve warm.

SWEETS

Caramelised apricots with rosewater syrup

Keep any leftover syrup in a sealed jar in the fridge. It's gorgeous spooned over a panna cotta such as the one on page 119, or make your own baklava and drizzle the syrup over the top after baking. You can also use it for poaching fruit or simply pour it over ice cream.

100 g soft brown sugar
4 large apricots, halved, pitted
1 tablespoon sherry vinegar
50 ml orange juice
slivered pistachios and micro
    herbs (optional), to serve

ROSEWATER SYRUP
200 ml water
200 g white sugar
1 tablespoon rosewater

1 For the rosewater syrup, combine the water, sugar and rosewater in a saucepan and bring to the boil over low heat, stirring until the sugar has dissolved. Simmer for 4–5 minutes or until reduced and syrupy. Remove from the heat and set aside. (Any leftover syrup will keep in an airtight container in the fridge for up to 1 month.)

2 Heat the sugar in a heavy-based frying pan over high heat for 5 minutes or until just melted and caramelised, taking care not to let it burn. Put the apricots into the caramelised sugar, cut-side down, and cook for 3–4 minutes or until well-coated in caramel. Add the sherry vinegar and orange juice and continue to cook for 1 minute, tossing gently to coat.

3 Serve the apricots in shallow bowls, drizzled with a little rosewater syrup and scattered with pistachios and micro herbs (if using).

Rhubarb and melamakarona crumble

Melomakarona are classic Greek honey biscuits, popular at Christmastime but also eaten year round. Somewhere between sweet and savoury, with a little hint of spice, they're like a Greek version of gingerbread. I like crumbling the biscuits over baked rhubarb for dessert. Alternatively, you can top rhubarb with the melomakarona batter and bake it in the oven like a traditional fruit crumble.

12 stalks rhubarb, trimmed, washed,
    cut into 14 cm lengths
150 g caster sugar
150 g honey
150 ml water

MELOMAKARONA CRUMBLE
50 g soft unsalted butter
20 g icing sugar
¼ cup (60 ml) olive oil
2 tablespoons freshly squeezed
    orange juice
pinch of ground clove
pinch of ground nutmeg
25 g ground walnuts, toasted,
    finely ground
¼ teaspoon ground cinnamon
2 teaspoons brandy
1 cup (150 g) plain flour
¼ teaspoon baking powder
2 tablespoons flaked almonds

1 Preheat the oven to 140°C fan-forced (160°C conventional).

2 Put the rhubarb into a roasting pan and cover with sugar, honey and water. Cover with foil and bake for 25–30 minutes or until soft and tender. Carefully drain the liquid, then transfer the rhubarb to a 1 litre-capacity baking dish so it snuggly fits in 1 layer.

3 Meanwhile, for the melomakarona batter, using hand-held electric beaters, cream the butter and icing sugar until pale and fluffy. Add the olive oil, orange juice, clove, nutmeg, walnuts, cinnamon and brandy. Mix well. Add the flour and baking powder and beat until smooth.

4 Increase the oven temperature to 170°C fan-forced (190°C conventional).

5 Put the melomakarona mixture onto a baking tray lined with baking paper. Using the palms of your hands, press the mixture into a 1 cm-thick disc. Bake for 20–25 minutes or until golden. Remove from the oven and, when cool enough to handle, break up and scatter over rhubarb, then scatter with flaked almonds. Pop back in the oven for 5 minutes or until just warm. Serve immediately.

Chocolate, walnut and salty caramel tart

This is my playful take on the Snickers bar, but I use walnuts instead of peanuts. Let the tart come to room temperature before you eat it.

1 quantity Sweet Pastry (see page 137)
110 g dark couverture chocolate
(70 per cent cocoa solids, see
page 140), finely chopped
40 g cold unsalted butter, chopped
½ cup (125 ml) thickened cream
2 teaspoons liquid glucose (see page 141)

WALNUT PRALINE
100 g walnuts
½ cup (110 g) caster sugar

SALTY CARAMEL SAUCE
200 ml pouring cream
180 g liquid glucose
180 g caster sugar
2 teaspoons sea salt flakes
180 g unsalted butter, chopped

1 Preheat the oven to 160°C fan-forced (180°C conventional).

2 For the walnut praline, bake the walnuts on a baking tray for 6–8 minutes or until lightly toasted. Remove and wrap in a clean tea towel, then rub to remove as much of the skins as possible. Transfer to a clean baking tray. Heat the sugar in a heavy-based saucepan over low heat, without stirring, but tilting the pan occasionally, for 10 minutes or until a dark but not burnt caramel forms. Pour the caramel over the nuts; make sure you cover each nut. Set aside to cool. Once set, break the praline onto a tea towel lined with baking paper, then wrap. Smash with a rolling pin until coarsely crushed. Set aside.

3 Roll the pastry dough between 2 sheets of baking paper until 5 mm thick. Line a shallow 24 cm tart tin with a removable base with the pastry, trimming off any excess. Prick the pastry with a fork. Refrigerate for 30 minutes.

4 Preheat the oven to 170°C fan-forced (190°C conventional). Line the pastry shell with baking paper and top with pastry weights or dried beans. Blind bake for 15 minutes. Remove the baking paper and pastry weights or beans, then reduce the temperature to 160°C fan-forced (180°C) and bake for another 10 minutes or until golden and dry.

5 For the sauce, bring the cream to the boil in a small saucepan over medium–high heat. Put the glucose, sugar, salt and butter into another saucepan and heat over medium heat until the mixture registers 147°C on a sugar thermometer (see page 141), stirring occasionally to prevent the mixture from catching. Add the hot cream to the glucose mixture and stir over low heat until incorporated. Remove the sauce from the heat. Set aside until just warm.

6 Meanwhile, put the chocolate and butter into a heatproof bowl. Bring the cream and glucose to the boil in a small saucepan over medium heat. Pour it over the chocolate and butter, let it stand for 5 minutes, then stir until melted and smooth.

7 Sprinkle walnut praline over the cooled pastry shell, then cover with a layer of caramel sauce. Leave for a few minutes to settle, then pour the chocolate mixture over the caramel sauce so it reaches the top of the tin. Refrigerate for 1 hour or until the chocolate mixture is firm. Serve at room temperature.

Creme brulee

I will never forget this recipe as it was one of the many basics I had to master when I started my chef training. This simple classic is always a hit when it reaches the table.

600 ml thickened cream
1 vanilla pod, split lengthways,
    seeds scraped
6 egg yolks
¼ cup (55 g) caster sugar, plus
    extra for topping

1 Preheat the oven to 120°C fan-forced (140°C conventional).

2 Heat the cream, vanilla pod and seeds in a small saucepan over medium heat to just below simmering point; do not let it boil. Remove the vanilla pod.

3 Using an electric mixer, whisk the egg yolks and caster sugar until thick and pale yellow. With the motor running, slowly add the hot cream and continue to whisk until combined.

4 Strain the mixture through a fine-mesh sieve into a jug (this removes any bubbles so the surface of the brulee is smooth). Put six shallow 125 ml-capacity moulds into a large deep roasting pan and pour the mixture into the moulds. Pull out the oven shelf and carefully place the pan on the shelf. Carefully add boiling water to the roasting pan to come halfway up the sides of the ramekins. Cover the pan loosely with foil.

5 Bake the brulees for 45 minutes or until the custard has just set (wobble one gently to check that the liquid has set). Carefully remove the roasting pan from the oven and place on a work surface. Carefully remove the moulds from the pan of hot water. Refrigerate the brulees for at least 1 hour.

6 Just before serving, sprinkle extra sugar evenly over the custards. Place under a hot grill for a few minutes to melt the sugar and caramelise the tops. (Alternatively, carefully use a kitchen blowtorch to caramelise the sugar.)

Chocolate olive-oil mousse

I stole the idea for this gorgeous recipe from Stelios, a very close friend of mine and an amazing pastry chef based in Athens. There are only three simple ingredients here: chocolate, olive oil and whipped cream. No eggs, no flour. Make this and eat it straight away – don't put it in the fridge.

100 g dark couverture chocolate (55 per cent cocoa solids, see page 140), finely chopped
50 g dark couverture chocolate (70 per cent cocoa solids, see page 140), finely chopped
100 ml extra virgin olive oil
1 cup (250 ml) double cream

1 Gently melt the chocolate in a heatproof bowl over a saucepan of simmering water, making sure the base of the bowl does not touch the water. Remove the bowl of melted chocolate from the heat and stir in the olive oil. Set aside.

2 Whisk the cream until soft peaks form. Add the whipped cream to the chocolate and olive oil mixture, then gently fold to mix well. Serve immediately.

Mastic meringues with pomegranate syrup

This is a fabulous Saturday-night dessert to serve to your friends and really show off. It's not that hard to cook either – it's just a matter of gathering the right ingredients and taking the time.

2 cups (500 ml) pouring cream
2 tablespoons icing sugar
mixed berries (such as blueberries, raspberries and strawberries) and Persian fairy floss (available from selected delicatessens and specialty food stores), to serve

MASTIC MERINGUES
½ cup (110 g) caster sugar
½ cup (110 g) soft brown sugar
2 mastic beads (see page 141)
4 egg whites
1 teaspoon lemon juice
2 teaspoons cornflour

POMEGRANATE SYRUP
¼ cup (55 g) caster sugar
¼ cup (60 ml) water
2 tablespoons pomegranate molasses

1 Preheat the oven to 175°C fan-forced (195°C conventional). Place the oven shelves on the lowest and middle rungs. Line 2 baking trays with baking paper.

2 For the mastic meringues, sift the sugars into a bowl. Crush the mastic beads and 2 tablespoons of the sugar with a mortar and pestle until finely ground, then stir into the sugar. Using an electric mixer, whisk the egg whites until soft peaks form (the bowl needs to be clean and dry for best results). Continue whisking the egg whites, adding the sugar a spoonful at a time, until firm glossy peaks form. Whisk in the lemon juice. Sift the cornflour over the egg-white mixture, then gently fold in with a flexible spatula to incorporate well.

3 Fill a piping bag fitted with a 1 cm plain nozzle with the meringue mixture. Pipe 5 cm rounds of meringue at 3 cm intervals on the prepared trays.

4 Put the trays into the oven and immediately reduce the temperature to 120°C fan-forced (140°C conventional). Bake the meringues for 50 minutes. Turn off the heat and leave the meringues to cool completely in the oven with a wooden spoon wedged in the door to keep it slightly ajar. (The cooked meringues will keep in an airtight container for up to 2 weeks.)

5 For the pomegranate syrup, put the sugar and water into a small saucepan and bring to the boil over low heat, stirring to dissolve the sugar. Set aside. (You will need 2 tablespoons.) Mix the pomegranate molasses with the sugar syrup, stirring to combine well.

6 Whisk the cream and icing sugar until soft peaks form. Cover and refrigerate until required.

7 When ready to serve, spoon the whipped cream into glasses and top with berries, then drizzle with the pomegranate syrup. Serve with the meringues and Persian fairy floss to the side.

Chocolate baklava

The argument still rages as to who invented baklava – the Turks, the Greeks or perhaps the Persians. Who cares? I have added chocolate to this baklava recipe just because I love chocolate and nuts together. These gorgeous little parcels are best eaten on the day they are made.

250 g slivered almonds, chopped
150 g honey, plus extra for drizzling
125 g dark couverture chocolate buttons
**   (see page 140)**
2 teaspoons ground cinnamon
6 sheets filo pastry
50 ml clarified butter (see page 140), melted

1 Preheat the oven to 180°C fan-forced (200°C conventional).

2 Put the almonds, honey, chocolate and cinnamon into a bowl, then stir to combine and set aside.

3 Lay 1 sheet of the filo on a clean bench. Brush the filo with butter, then fold in half and brush again with butter. Spread one-sixth of the almond mixture along the short edge of the filo. Fold in the sides to cover the filling, then roll up tightly. Place the filo parcel seam-side-down on a baking tray lined with baking paper. Repeat this process with the remaining pastry, butter and filling.

4 Bake the baklava for 6 minutes or until golden and crisp. Leave to cool, then drizzle with extra honey and serve.

Fruit and nut parfait

This is a sophisticated version of the mass-produced fruit and nut chocolate bar sold in milk bars and supermarkets. You'll need to start making this at least two days in advance. The dried fruit needs to be soaked in sherry overnight, then the parfait needs to be frozen in a terrine mould overnight to firm.

75 g prunes, pitted, diced
75 g fresh dates, pitted, diced
100 g dried apricots, diced
⅓ cup (80 ml) Pedro Ximenez sherry
    (see page 141)
450 ml pouring cream
50 g blanched almonds
6 egg yolks
150 g caster sugar
185 ml water
30 g pistachios, roughly chopped

1 Put the prunes, dates and apricots into a small bowl. Pour over the sherry and stir to mix. Cover with plastic film and soak overnight. Drain.

2 The next day, whisk the cream with hand-held electric beaters until soft peaks form, then set aside.

3 Preheat the oven to 180°C fan-forced (200°C conventional). Roast the almonds on a baking tray until light golden, about 8 minutes. Roughly chop and set aside.

4 Line a 1 litre-capacity terrine mould (mine is 24 cm × 8 cm) with plastic film, leaving some overhanging to help you remove the parfait from the mould when it has set.

5 Using an electric mixer, whisk the egg yolks until just mixed.

6 Put the sugar and water into a small saucepan over medium heat, then bring to a simmer, stirring to dissolve the sugar. Cook until the syrup reaches thread stage (it should register 110°C on a sugar thermometer, see page 141). (If judging when the syrup is ready by eye, look for small, equal-sized bubbles over the surface when the syrup is ready.) With the electric mixer running, gradually pour the hot syrup in a slow, steady stream onto the egg yolks, whisking continuously. Continue to whisk until the mixture doubles in volume and has cooled to room temperature.

7 Gently fold in the whipped cream and combine well. Fold through the drained fruit, almonds and pistachios, taking care that they are dispersed evenly throughout the mixture. Transfer to the prepared terrine mould and spread out evenly. Cover with plastic film and freeze overnight.

8 Cut into slices and serve immediately.

Apple tarts with frangipane cream

Frangipane is a rich pastry cream flavoured with almonds. The puff pastry base must be cooked at a high temperature so that the air trapped between the layers expands and causes the pastry to rise. The fat content separates the layers, giving the pastry a crisp texture.

2 sheets frozen butter puff pastry, thawed
1 egg yolk, lightly beaten
2 small apples, peeled, cored, quartered,
    thinly sliced
⅓ cup (115 g) orange marmalade (optional)

FRANGIPANE CREAM
100 g unsalted butter, softened
100 g caster sugar
100 g ground almonds
1 egg
½ teaspoon vanilla extract

1 For the frangipane cream, process the butter, sugar and ground almonds in a food processor until blended well. Add the egg and vanilla extract and process until well mixed. Set aside.

2 Preheat the oven to 180°C fan-forced (200°C conventional).

3 Cut each pastry sheet into four 10 cm rounds using a 10 cm pastry cutter or saucer as a guide. Put the pastry rounds onto 2 baking trays lined with baking paper. Score a 1 cm border around the edge of each pastry round with a sharp knife, taking care not to cut all the way through the pastry. Brush the pastry with the egg yolk to glaze. Put 2 teaspoons of the frangipane cream onto the centre of each piece of pastry and spread to the border, forming a 5 mm-thick layer. Place the apple slices on top of the frangipane cream.

4 Bake the tarts for 10 minutes, then reduce the temperature to 160°C fan-forced (180°C conventional) and bake for a further 15–20 minutes or until the pastry is golden brown and puffed around the edges. Remove the tarts from the oven and transfer to a wire rack to cool.

5 Put the marmalade (if using) into a microwave-safe bowl and microwave on medium power for 20 seconds to warm. Brush the tarts with warmed marmalade to glaze, if desired. Serve.

Passionfruit jellies

I especially love the tartness and sweetness of homemade passionfruit jelly. If preferred, use two 170 g tins passionfruit pulp and strain to yield 200 ml juice. By the way, it might sound strange, but place some of this jelly on top of a freshly shucked oyster and you'll discover an amazing combination of flavours and textures.

3 teaspoons gelatine powder
½ cup (125 ml) boiling water
200 ml strained passionfruit pulp (from about 14 passionfruit)
1 cup (250 ml) strained fresh orange juice
⅓ cup (75 g) caster sugar, plus extra if needed
raspberries (optional), to serve

1 Whisk the gelatine and water in a bowl until the gelatine has dissolved. Put the passionfruit pulp and orange juice into a small saucepan and warm over low heat, then add the sugar and gelatine mixture and stir to combine until the sugar has dissolved. Taste the mixture and check if you need to sweeten it with extra sugar. Remove the pan from the heat and pour the mixture into a heatproof jug.

2 Divide the jelly mixture among four 140 ml-capacity jelly moulds and refrigerate for 3 hours or until set.

3 To unmould the jellies, briefly dip the moulds into a bowl of hot water, then turn upside down onto small serving plates and shake gently to release the jelly. Serve with raspberries, if you like.

Chocolate marshmallow souffles

Making a souffle is so rewarding. There's such a sense of achievement, especially when it rises nicely and is soft and gooey in the middle. Lots of people are scared of making souffles. The trick is to not overbeat the whites. Use a large metal spoon to gently fold the whites into the rest of the mixture: the result will be lovely and light.

softened butter, for greasing
2 tablespoons caster sugar, plus extra
    for dusting
200 g dark couverture chocolate
    buttons (see page 140)
2 tablespoons milk or pouring cream
3 eggs, separated
2 egg whites
4 tablespoons mini marshmallows,
    plus extra to serve (optional)
icing sugar, for dusting

1 Preheat the oven to 200°C fan-forced (220°C conventional).

2 Grease four 200-ml capacity souffle moulds with softened butter, then dust with a little caster sugar. Shake out any excess sugar, then wipe the top inside edge of each mould clean with paper towel or a clean tea towel. Set aside on a baking tray.

3 Place the chocolate in a microwave-safe bowl. Microwave on medium power for 2 minutes, then remove and stir with a metal spoon. Leave for a few minutes; the residual heat will continue to melt the chocolate. Set the melted chocolate aside to cool slightly, then stir in the milk or cream and the egg yolks.

4 Using an electric mixer, whisk the 5 egg whites until soft peaks form, then gradually add the sugar, whisking continuously until firm white peaks form. Do not overbeat. Using a large metal spoon, fold one-third of the beaten egg whites into the chocolate mixture to help loosen the mix. Fold in the remaining beaten egg whites.

5 Place 1 tablespoon of mini-marshmallows in the base of each souffle mould. Spoon in the chocolate mixture and wipe around the inside edge to make sure it is clean (this helps the souffles to rise). Bake the souffles for 14 minutes or until risen and just cooked.

6 Dust the souffles with icing sugar and serve immediately with extra marshmallows, if desired.

Strawberry and ouzo sorbet with buffalo-yoghurt panna cotta

SERVES 8

This dish is all about simplicity and elegance. The ouzo adds a lovely anise flavour to the strawberry sorbet, while the buffalo yoghurt is super-creamy and offers a great balance to the sorbet. You'll need a sugar thermometer to get the temperatures right.

400 g strawberries, hulled, halved
600 ml water
120 g liquid glucose (see page 141)
480 g caster sugar
2 teaspoons ouzo, or to taste
dill sprigs or fennel tops (optional),
    to serve

BUFFALO-YOGHURT PANNA COTTA
1 cup (250 ml) milk
½ cup (110 g) caster sugar
1 vanilla pod, split, seeds scraped
5 gold-strength gelatine leaves (see
    page 140)
800 ml buffalo yoghurt (if unavailable,
    use natural sheep's milk yoghurt)

1 Put the strawberries and water into a small saucepan and simmer for 5 minutes. Transfer to a blender and blend until smooth. Return the strawberry puree to the pan and add the glucose and sugar. Heat over medium heat until the mixture registers 85°C on a sugar thermometer (see page 141). Remove from the heat and add the ouzo, then press with a spoon through a fine-mesh sieve set over a bowl. Cover with plastic film and refrigerate until cool. Transfer the cooled strawberry mixture to an ice-cream machine, then churn and freeze following the manufacturer's instructions.

2 For the yoghurt panna cotta, heat the milk, sugar and vanilla seeds and pod in a saucepan over low heat until the sugar dissolves; it should register 60°C on the sugar thermometer.

3 Meanwhile, put the gelatine into a bowl of iced water for 5 minutes or until soft. Remove the gelatine, squeezing out any excess liquid, then stir it into the milk mixture and leave to cool. When it registers 30°C on the sugar thermometer, whisk in the yoghurt, then divide the mixture among eight 125 ml-capacity dariole moulds (see page 140) or pour into a large serving bowl. Refrigerate until set, approximately 3 hours.

4 Serve the panna cotta with spoonfuls of sorbet alongside and a sprig of dill or fennel to garnish, if desired.

Strawberries and vanilla cooked in a bag

This dish is incredibly easy. You can prepare the strawberries in the paper parcel well in advance so all you have to do is cook them just before you're ready to serve. The gentle heat brings out the flavour of the strawberries, and infuses them with vanilla. Make sure when you wash the strawberries that you don't drown them in water or they will lose their flavour.

250 g strawberries, hulled
1 vanilla pod, split, seeds scraped
1 tablespoon icing sugar
1 stick cinnamon
**clotted cream and oregano
    leaves (optional), to serve**

1 Preheat the oven to 170°C fan-forced (190°C conventional).

2 Cut a 30 cm square piece of baking paper. Place the strawberries in the middle of the paper. Scatter the vanilla seeds and pod over the strawberries. Sprinkle the sugar evenly over the top, then gently toss to coat. Add the cinnamon, then bring together the 4 corners of the paper and tie together with kitchen string so the parcel resembles a money bag. Bake for 12 minutes.

3 Open the bag, scatter with oregano leaves (if using) and serve the strawberries with clotted cream to the side.

Fig ice cream with sherry-muscatel compote

What's nice about this recipe is that you can use soft and bruised figs – the riper the better – to make the ice cream, and their leaves to serve it in. Don't freeze the fig leaves, though, as they'll deteriorate in the freezer.

2 cups (500 ml) full-cream milk
2 cups (500 ml) pouring cream
½ stick cinnamon
1 vanilla pod, split, seeds scraped
10 egg yolks
140 g caster sugar
300 g purple figs (about 4), stems
    trimmed, quartered
1½ tablespoons sherry vinegar
finely grated zest of 2 lemons
fig leaves, washed (optional), to serve

SHERRY-MUSCATEL COMPOTE
⅓ cup (75 g) caster sugar
1 tablespoon sherry vinegar
1 cup (250 ml) cream sherry
150 g muscatels

1 Heat the milk, cream, cinnamon, vanilla pod and seeds in a saucepan over low heat until just warmed through; do not allow to simmer. Remove from the heat and set aside for 10 minutes to infuse, then strain, discarding the cinnamon and vanilla.

2 Whisk the egg yolks and 100 g of the caster sugar together. Pour one-third of the warm milk mixture onto the egg-yolk mixture. Whisk well, then pour back into the pan with the warm milk mixture. Using a wooden spoon, stir the mixture continuously over low heat for 10 minutes or until it coats the back of the spoon. Cover the custard mixture closely with plastic film and refrigerate to cool.

3 Meanwhile, put the figs, remaining sugar, sherry vinegar and lemon zest into a small saucepan and bring to a simmer. Reduce the heat to low and cook, stirring occasionally, for 45 minutes or until thick and jammy. Transfer to a blender and blend until smooth. Set aside to cool.

4 Add the cooled fig puree to the custard. Transfer the mixture to an ice-cream machine, then churn and freeze following the manufacturer's instructions.

5 Meanwhile, for the sherry-muscatel compote, put the sugar, vinegar and sherry into a saucepan over low heat, and stir until the sugar has dissolved. Add the muscatels. Cook the syrup for a further 18 minutes over low heat; do not allow it to boil. Remove from the heat and set aside to cool.

6 Serve the ice cream with the sherry-muscatel compote to the side. (For special occasions, wrap servings of ice cream in fig leaves and tie with raffia – each diner then unwraps the parcel at the table).

Triple-chocolate muffins

These rich yet light muffins are perfect for sharing. The addition of white chocolate balls creates a molten centre that chocoholics like me just love.

1¾ cups (260 g) self-raising flour
½ cup (50 g) dutch-process cocoa
    (see page 140), sifted
¾ cup (165 g) soft brown sugar
1 cup (250 ml) milk
½ cup (125 ml) vegetable oil
2 eggs, lightly beaten
1 teaspoon vanilla extract
100 g dark couverture chocolate buttons
    (see page 140)
12 white chocolate balls (I use Lindt)
    or white chocolate buttons

1 Preheat the oven to 170°C fan-forced (190°C conventional). Line a 12-hole muffin pan with paper cases (or use 12 silicone muffin moulds, as in the photo here).

2 Combine the flour, cocoa and sugar in a large bowl. Mix the milk, oil, egg and vanilla in a medium-sized bowl. Pour the milk mixture into the flour mixture and gently stir until just combined; don't over-mix or the muffins will be tough. Fold in the dark chocolate, then spoon the batter into the muffin cases until they are three-quarters full. Add a white chocolate ball or button to each case and top with a little more of the muffin batter.

3 Bake the muffins for 25 minutes or until firm to the touch. Put the muffins onto a wire rack and set aside to cool. (The muffins will keep in an airtight container for up to 3 days.)

Salty caramel sweets

The combination of salt and caramel seems to be flavour of the month. It's great to be able to give kids sweets that are handmade instead of stuff out of a packet – and it's a nice treat for the big kids too!

4 g sea salt flakes
100 g unsalted butter, softened
50 g dark couverture chocolate (70 per cent
    cocoa solids, see page 140), finely chopped
240 g caster sugar
80 g liquid glucose (see page 141)
2 tablespoons water
¾ cup (180 ml) double cream

1 Line a 20 × 15 cm baking dish with baking paper.

2 Stir the salt into the softened butter to combine well. Cover with plastic film and refrigerate to chill and firm.

3 Half-fill a small saucepan with water and bring to the boil. Reduce the heat to low. Put the chocolate into a heatproof bowl that fits snugly over the saucepan, making sure the bottom of the bowl does not touch the water. Stir to melt the chocolate, then remove the pan from the heat and set aside.

4 Put the sugar, glucose and water into another saucepan over medium heat, stirring to dissolve the sugar. Bring to the boil without stirring again. Cook the mixture until it turns light golden, then immediately remove from the heat and add the cream and chilled butter mixture – take care as the mixture may spit. Return the pan to the heat and cook until the mixture registers 118°C on a sugar thermometer (see page 141). Immediately remove the pan from the heat and stir in the melted chocolate until just combined.

5 Pour the caramel mixture into the prepared baking dish. Leave the mixture to set at room temperature, then refrigerate until firm, about 1 hour.

6 Using a sharp knife, cut the salted caramel into 3 cm × 1.5 cm pieces. Wrap the pieces in squares of clear cellophane, twisting the ends to seal. (Store the salted caramels in an airtight container in the fridge for up to 1 week.)

Yoghurt and lemon syrup cake

This lovely, moist cake has a delicious lemony tang and is great served with a pot of tea. To ensure the cake absorbs the syrup, pour it over while the cake is still hot. Although this is terrific eaten while still warm, it just gets better with age.

125 g unsalted butter, softened
250 g caster sugar
2 eggs
1 cup (280 g) natural thick Greek-style yoghurt
1 teaspoon vanilla extract
finely grated zest of 2 lemons
¼ cup (60 ml) lemon juice
2⅔ cups (400 g) self-raising flour
½ teaspoon bicarbonate of soda

LEMON SYRUP
1 cup (220 g) caster sugar
1 cup (250 ml) water
⅓ cup (80 ml) lemon juice
2 lemons, well scrubbed, thinly
    sliced widthways

1 Preheat the oven to 180°C fan-forced (200°C conventional). Grease and line a 23 cm springform cake tin with baking paper.

2 Cream the butter and sugar in an electric mixer until light and fluffy. Add the eggs, one at a time, beating well after adding each one, then continue to mix until combined. Add the yoghurt, vanilla, lemon zest and juice and continue to mix. Gently fold the flour and bicarbonate of soda through with a flexible spatula.

3 Spoon the batter into the prepared cake tin and smooth the surface with the back of a large metal spoon; the mixture will be quite firm.

4 Bake for 45 minutes or until the cake is cooked through – a skewer inserted in the centre should come out clean.

5 Meanwhile, for the lemon syrup, combine the sugar, water and lemon juice in a small saucepan and cook over low heat, stirring with a wooden spoon to dissolve the sugar. Add the lemon slices and simmer for 10 minutes to soften the lemon. Set aside to cool.

6 Remove the cake from the oven and poke it all over with a bamboo skewer to make lots of small holes; this helps the syrup soak into the cake. Slowly pour the cooled lemon syrup over the hot cake until it has been absorbed. Decorate the top of the cake with candied lemon slices. Leave the cake to cool in the tin.

7 Remove the cake from the tin, slice and serve. (Leftover cake will keep in an airtight container for up to 1 week.)

Mini chocolate tsoureki with hot chocolate

This is my take on tsoureki, the traditional brioche-style Greek Easter bread. Here I have added chocolate, just because I love it. Dip slices of the bread into the hot chocolate for a really indulgent treat.

10 g dried yeast (see page 141)
90 g caster sugar
100 ml milk, warmed
1⅔ cups (250 g) '00' flour (see page 140), plus extra for dusting
⅓ cup (30 g) dutch-process cocoa (see page 140)
table salt
2 eggs
50 g soft unsalted butter, chopped
½ cup (95 g) dark couverture chocolate buttons (see page 140)
olive oil, for greasing

HOT CHOCOLATE
100 ml milk
400 ml pouring cream
300 g dark couverture chocolate buttons (see page 140)

1 Mix the yeast with 1 teaspoon of the sugar and the warm milk in a medium-sized bowl. Sift the flour and cocoa into another bowl. Add 75 g of the flour mixture to the yeast mixture. Cover with plastic film and stand in a warm place for 15 minutes or until it is spongey.

2 Put the remaining flour mixture, sugar and 1 teaspoon salt into an electric mixer fitted with a dough hook. Add the yeast mixture and eggs. Mix on low speed for 6 minutes. Add the butter, piece by piece, beating until smooth. Place the dough in an oiled bowl, cover with plastic film and leave in a warm place for 1½ hours or until doubled in size.

3 Grease 6 mini loaf tins (mine are 10 × 6 cm) and line them with baking paper. Turn the dough out onto a floured bench, then knock it back with your fists to remove any air. Add the chocolate buttons and knead to incorporate. Using a sharp knife, divide the dough into 6 pieces, then roll into balls. Transfer the balls to the prepared tins. Cover the loaf tins with a damp tea towel and set aside in a warm place for 30 minutes or until doubled in size.

4 Preheat the oven to 190°C fan-forced (210°C conventional).

5 Put the loaf tins onto a baking tray and bake for 20 minutes or until a skewer inserted in the centre of the tsoureki comes out clean. Remove each loaf from its tin and leave to cool on a wire rack.

6 For the hot chocolate, heat the milk and cream in a small saucepan over medium heat until warm. Add the chocolate and remove the pan from the heat. Stir until the chocolate has melted. Serve with the tsoureki.

BASICS

Chicken stock

1.5 kg chicken bones, including backs and necks
(about 6 carcasses), washed, roughly chopped
750 g chicken wings, separated at the joint
1 onion, roughly chopped
1 stick celery, roughly chopped
1 leek, white part only, well-washed, sliced
6 stems flat-leaf parsley
2 stems thyme
1 fresh bay leaf
10 black peppercorns
about 4 litres water

1 Put the washed chicken bones and wings, onion, celery, leek, parsley, thyme, bay leaf and peppercorns into a large stockpot, then add enough cold water to cover by at least 2 cm. Bring to the simmer, then reduce the heat to low and maintain the stock at a constant gentle simmer for 3 hours, topping up with water occasionally, if necessary, to keep all the ingredients submerged. Skim any foam and scum regularly from the surface for the first 30 minutes. (Skimming the surface and keeping the stock at a simmer results in a clear stock. Boiling results in a cloudy stock.)

2 Set aside for 30 minutes, then strain the stock through a colander lined with damp muslin into a clean container. Chill in the fridge overnight. Remove the solidified fat from the surface. (The stock can be refrigerated in a labelled and dated airtight container for up to 3 days or frozen for up to 3 months.)

Mayonnaise

2 egg yolks
2 teaspoons white wine vinegar
2 teaspoons dijon mustard
1 cup (250 ml) vegetable oil
sea salt flakes and freshly ground white pepper

1 Put the egg yolks, vinegar and mustard in a small bowl. Using a stick blender, blend until well mixed. Gradually pour in the oil, drop by drop at first and then in a slow, steady stream, blending continuously until all the oil is incorporated and the mayonnaise emulsifies. Season to taste with salt and pepper. (Store in an airtight container in the fridge for up to 1 week.)

Pasta dough

1⅔ cups (250 g) '00' flour (see page 140),
    plus extra for dusting
2 × 55 g eggs, lightly beaten
3 egg yolks (from 55 g eggs)
2 teaspoons extra virgin olive oil
semolina, for dusting

1 Pulse the flour in a food processor for 30 seconds. While the motor is running, add the egg, then the egg yolks and olive oil. Keep processing until the mixture is the consistency of coarse breadcrumbs. Shape into a ball, wrap with plastic film and leave to rest for 2 hours at room temperature.

2 Cut the pasta dough in half. Working with one piece at a time, feed the dough through the rollers of a pasta machine set at its widest setting, turning the handle and teasing the rolled dough along the bench as it feeds through the machine. Fold one end over onto the centre and press it down. Fold the other end over the top and press it down, then feed the dough through the machine on the same setting. Repeat this process twice. Fold the dough and feed it through the rollers, reducing the setting each time, making the dough thinner, until you reach the second-last setting. Cut the pasta sheet in half, then cover with a tea towel. Repeat with the remaining dough to make 4 pasta sheets.

3 Use to make ravioli (see page 58), lasagne or other filled pasta, or simply cut into the desired shapes.

Filo pastry

1⅔ cups (250 g) plain flour, plus extra for dusting
sea salt flakes
⅔ cup (160 ml) lukewarm water (about 32°C)
2 tablespoons olive oil, plus extra for greasing
cornflour, for dusting

1 Mix the flour and a pinch of salt in an electric mixer fitted with a dough hook on low–medium speed. With the motor running, gradually pour in the water, then gradually add the olive oil, continuing to mix for 10 minutes or until a soft, smooth and pliable dough forms; this is a moist dough. Transfer the dough to a lightly oiled bowl Cover with plastic film and set aside for 2 hours.

2 Divide the dough into 10 even-sized pieces, then cover with a clean, damp tea towel. Working with one piece of dough at a time, dust your hands with cornflour, then roll the dough into a small ball. Pass the dough through the second widest setting of a pasta machine, turning the handle and teasing the rolled dough along the bench as it feeds through the machine. Repeat feeding the dough through the rollers, reducing the setting a notch each time until you reach the second last setting, dusting the dough with more cornflour if necessary to prevent it from sticking to the rollers. Cut the dough in half so that it is easier to pass through the rollers. Pass each piece of dough through the final setting. Place the rolled dough on a lightly floured tea towel. Cover with another clean, damp tea towel. (Have another person assist, if possible.)

3 Proceed with the recipe immediately.

Maggie Beer's
sour-cream pastry

200 g chilled butter, chopped
1⅔ cups (250 g) plain flour, plus extra
    for dusting
½ cup (120 g) sour cream
1 egg yolk

1 Process the butter, flour, sour cream and egg yolk in a food processor until a dough forms. Form into a ball and flatten slightly. Wrap in plastic film and refrigerate for 20 minutes.

2 Proceed with the recipe.

Sweet pastry

300 g soft unsalted butter, chopped
150 g caster sugar
seeds from ½ vanilla pod
3 cups (450 g) plain flour, plus extra
    for dusting
1 egg, lightly beaten
1 tablespoon thickened cream

1 Beat the butter, sugar and vanilla seeds in an electric mixer on its lowest speed until smooth and creamy (not pale and fluffy); do not overbeat. Add the flour, egg and cream and beat until smooth and the mixture just comes together in a ball; take care not to overwork. Shape the dough into a disc, divide in half, then wrap one half in plastic film and freeze for later use. Wrap the other half in plastic film and refrigerate for 1 hour.

2 Proceed with the recipe.

Glossary

Asian spiral vegetable cutter
Used to cut vegetables into spirals. Available from Asian food stores.

Carnaroli rice
An Italian medium-grain rice. I prefer it when making risotto as its grains are longer with a firmer texture and more starch than arborio rice.

Cartouche
A piece of baking paper placed directly on the contents of a saucepan or casserole dish to help retain moisture during or after cooking.

Citric acid
This weak acidulant occurs naturally in some vegetables and fruits, especially citrus fruits such as lemons and limes. Available in powder form from larger supermarkets, it is used to preserve foods and add a sour taste.

Clarified butter
Pop unsalted butter into a microwave-safe container and microwave on medium power for 90 seconds. Remove and allow the milk solids and butterfat to separate. Skim off the butterfat and reserve, discarding the milk solids – this golden liquid is clarified butter.

Cocoa – dutch-process
Unsweetened cocoa powder treated with an alkali to neutralise its acids, resulting in a more rounded chocolate-y flavour.

Couverture chocolate – dark
Chocolate must contain at least 32 per cent cocoa butter and 54 per cent combined total of cocoa solids and cocoa butter to be classified as couverture. The higher percentage of cocoa butter and solids a chocolate contains, the less sugar, and, as a result the more intense the flavour. Available in blocks and buttons from specialty food stores and good delis.

Dariole moulds
Round or oval-shaped stainless steel or heatproof plastic moulds used to give desserts such as creme caramel and puddings a uniform shape and size. Available from specialty cookware stores.

Fine-mesh sieve
Made from fine stainless-steel mesh, this is an indispensable tool for straining effectively.

Fish tweezers
Used to remove small (pin) bones from fish fillets. Their precise-fitting ends are designed to maximise their grip on small bones and pull them out without affecting the texture or appearance of the fish.

Flour – 'oo'
A super-fine Italian grade of flour used for making pasta. Available from larger supermarkets, specialty food stores and good delis.

Freekeh
A grain made from wheat harvested while still young that is sun-dried, carefully set on fire to separate the straw and chaff from the seeds, then roasted and threshed into smaller pieces. Available from specialty food stores, larger supermarkets and health food stores.

Gelatine
A setting agent derived from collagen that comes in leaf and powder form used to set jellies, mousses and sweets. The leaves are available in different grades based on how easily they set: titanium-strength leaves have the strongest setting ability and silver have the weakest, with gold somewhere in between. The leaves must be soaked in cold water to soften prior to use. It is important to use the strength of leave specified in a recipe for optimum results. The recipes in this book call for gold-strength leaves. Available from specialty food stores and good delis.

Haloumi cheese
A Cypriot-style cheese traditionally made from goat's and sheep's milk with a high melting point, making it suitable for grilling and frying. Available from larger supermarkets and good delis.

Kefalograviera cheese
Originating in Greece, this hard, salty cheese is traditionally made from sheep's milk and is commonly used for cooking, although it is also appreciated as a table cheese. Available from Greek food stores and good delis.

Liquid glucose
A 'simple' sugar in syrup form commonly used in commercial kitchens for making ice cream, sorbet and confectionary. It often replaces a proportion of regular white sugar in recipes. Available from health food stores and some supermarkets.

Mastic beads
The hardened, opaque edible resin from an evergreen tree that grows in Chios, Greece, this is used in Greek baking, sweets, drinks and ice cream. Available from Greek food stores, good delis and herbies.com.au.

Salted white cod roe paste
Salted and cured cod roe used to make the Greek dip taramosalata. Available from Greek food stores and good delis.

Samos vin doux
This fortified Greek dessert wine hails from the island of Samos. If unavailable, substitute with a classic dessert muscat.

Sherry – Pedro Ximénez
A rich sweet dark sherry made from Pedro Ximenez grapes from the Jerez region of Spain.

Simmer mat
A simmer mat is placed between the heat source and pan to regulate and maintain a steady low heat to prevent food from sticking to the base of the pan.

Smoked paprika
A Spanish spice made from a variety of capsicum that is slowly smoked over oak and sold in three varieties – hot, bittersweet and sweet. Used sparingly, it adds a fantastic smoky and complex flavour. Available from specialty food stores and good delis.

Sugar thermometer
A thermometer used to measure the temperature of sugar syrups, caramel and confectionery. It can also be used to test whether jam has reached setting point and to check the temperature of oil for deep-frying.

Yeast
A dried or fresh leavening agent used to convert sugar to alcohol (for beer and wine) or water and carbon dioxide when making bread and other baked goods. When fresh yeast is unavailable, substitute half the quantity of active dried yeast. Fresh and dried yeast should be stored in the fridge and used before the use-by date. Fresh yeast is available from health food stores.

Index

LANTERN

Published by the Penguin Group
Penguin Group (Australia)
707 Collins Street, Melbourne, Victoria 3008, Australia
(a division of Pearson Australia Group Pty Ltd)
Penguin Group (USA) Inc.
375 Hudson Street, New York, New York 10014, USA
Penguin Group (Canada)
90 Eglinton Avenue East, Suite 700, Toronto, Canada ON M4P 2Y3
(a division of Pearson Penguin Canada Inc.)
Penguin Books Ltd
80 Strand, London WC2R 0RL, England
Penguin Ireland
25 St Stephen's Green, Dublin 2, Ireland
(a division of Penguin Books Ltd)
Penguin Books India Pvt Ltd
11 Community Centre, Panchsheel Park, New Delhi – 110 017, India
Penguin Group (NZ)
67 Apollo Drive, Rosedale, North Shore 0632, New Zealand
(a division of Pearson New Zealand Ltd)
Penguin Books (South Africa) (Pty) Ltd
24 Sturdee Avenue, Rosebank, Johannesburg 2196, South Africa

Penguin Books Ltd, Registered Offices: 80 Strand,
London, WC2R 0RL, England

First published by Penguin Group (Australia), 2012

10 9 8 7 6 5 4 3 2 1

Text copyright © George Calombaris 2012

Photographs copyright © Mark Chew

Design by Lantern Studio © Penguin Group (Australia)
Typeset in Alright Sans and Adobe Caslon
by Post Pre-press Group, Brisbane, Queensland
Colour reproduction by Splitting Image, Clayton, Victoria
Printed in China by Everbest Printing Co Ltd

National Library of Australia
Cataloguing-in-Publication data:

Calombaris, George.
George Calombaris / George Calombaris

9781921383120 (pbk.)

Lantern cookery classics.
Includes bibliographical references.

Cooking.

641.5

penguin.com.au/lantern